CODE OF PROFESSIONAL CONDUCT

Standards & Ethics
for the
Investigative Profession

Fourth Edition

KITTY HAILEY, CLI

KITTY HAILEY, CLI
614 South 4th Street #320
Philadelphia, PA 19147
www.kittyhailey.com

ISBN: 979-8-218-12031-3

Printed in the United States of America

Cover design by Katie Singh

A beacon of ethics and proper technique, Kitty has taken the entire industry on, from Alabama to Wyoming, and taught us what an ethical investigator looks like. "Do no harm" is the mantra for many of us, because it's succinct and purposeful, and when we traverse our often dangerous and uncharted work, it keeps us safe.

Cynthia Hetherington, President
The Hetherington Group

This new edition of Kitty's book should be on the desk of every investigator. Not using it as a resource is a risk to your personal and professional reputation.

H. Ellis Armistead
H. Ellis Armistead & Associates, LLC

Table of Contents

Foreword

When I started as a legal investigator over thirty years ago, I was amazed to discover few ethical guidelines for those in this profession.

Those of us working as legal investigators are constantly confronted with decisions on how to provide the best service for our clients and at the same time, accomplish those tasks ethically. Our profession and the people surrounding our profession provide ample opportunity for the unwary investigator to become involved in unethical and even illegal activity.

Over the years, various associations and, to a degree, some state licensing boards have produced ethical guidelines for legal and/or private investigators. Only Kitty Hailey's guidelines are recognized nationally throughout our profession.

I have known Kitty for over thirty years. In my practice, which is primarily criminal defense investigations, I am regularly confronted with scenarios that require me to make decisions regarding the ethical and often legal implications of a given task. Just because an activity is legal does not make it ethical.

The ever-changing legal and technological landscape necessitates constant, well-thought-out research.

I have frequently consulted with Kitty when making difficult decisions. There is no one in our profession who has given more thought and performed more research of the ethical guidelines for the legal investigator than Kitty Hailey.

H. Ellis Armistead
H. Ellis Armistead & Associates, LLC
Legal Investigations
Denver, Colorado

Preface

Times change. Ethics don't. With each passing year, changes in technology, ability and beliefs have a huge impact on the collective conscience of our world. Each new advance or altered concept brings with it another challenge to our profession. We are tasked with determining how to handle each situation as it is encountered. We are asked to perform work never before imagined. A changing world requires adaptation.

As information becomes increasingly free flowing, our duty is to be cognizant of the lines, however, blurred, between our ability to access data and our legal and moral right to use it.

The investigator is a resource for information. The goal is to provide assistance in a responsible and resourceful manner. No matter how much the world changes or abilities fluctuate, the Code still serves to guide the Investigator in doing his or her job in a manner that is consistent and considerate to society. It serves to advance the reputation of the profession and ensure that sufficient effort is afforded each client. Local, regional and national laws are ever changing. The investigator has the added responsibility of performing each assignment with a due diligent effort to abide by the Constitution and permissible laws.

This is the fourth edition and twentieth year of this writing. Some points have been amended, clarified and reworded to provide the best guidance possible. Most concepts included herein have not changed, as they were valid twenty years ago and are equally valid today. This writing deals with truthfulness, diligence, respect and honesty by investigators, toward investigators and to the public.

Times change. Our foundation is based in honest and diligent work performed in a professional manner for the benefit of all.

Acknowledgements

Since the writing of the last volume, I have lost loved ones, gained friends and seen the addition of new generations within my family. Each change affects my outlook on life. What remains constant are the values I was taught as a child. For this I thank my parents and acknowledge their everlasting influence. My sister Rose and brother John remain my greatest mentors, boosters and critics. I love them for that. I have been strengthened by each personal relationship. Now my greatest joy comes with the birth and growth of new additions to my diverse extended family. I hope that I pass along some of my ethic and value structure to each of them. My family is diverse and beautiful. I learn constantly from them and hope that I pass along to them my love and respect for humanity. They are good people and I am privileged to be a part of their lives.

My investigative family has grown. I see professionals all over the world as members of an amazing fraternity and sorority of hard working, caring and capable individuals. Together we solve problems, recover precious belongings, represent those incapable of helping themselves, assist in freeing the wrongfully convicted and locating missing or lost loved ones. You are my heroes. You do this work daily with little acknowledgment for your amazing skills. I value each of you and thank you for making me a better Investigator.

Now to the necessary acknowledgments:

The American Bar Association's Model Rules of Professional Conduct (RPC) has been used as a guide after which this volume is patterned. In many instances, wording has been extrapolated exactly from the RPC as it so aptly and appropriately applies to both attorneys and investigators. While investigators cannot and should not practice law, many of the ethical tenets that affect one profession are truly applicable in the other. Credit and thanks is given to the many individuals who have worked over the years to clarify the RPC and so intelligently define and refine its language. It is from this work that the form of the Code of Professional Conduct for investigators has been established. Full credit and grateful thanks are due to those who have so eloquently stated these principles before me.

It is also appropriate to acknowledge the large number of state, national and international associations whose codes of ethics were studied as the basis for this volume. The place of the private investigator in society has become elevated because of the interest each of these associations hold in the reputation and professionalism of their members. The codes of conduct of these many associations have become the grass roots structure upon which the Code of Professional Conduct has been built. These individual organizations and state regulatory statutes governing the licensing of investigators have been cited in a chart at the conclusion of this volume.

Introduction

This publication is designed to provide a guide for investigators working within the private sector. As of this time, there are no national standards for this profession. The goal of this author is to provide that standard with this writing. Individual states have opted either to require licensing or to not do so. This authority is granted through a variety of regulatory agencies. These agencies vary from police entities to licensing boards. The standards by which investigators are licensed are as individual as the states from which they hail. In some instances, licensing is performed by counties and not by the state, thus multiplying the possibilities for inconsistency in action and enforcement.

Investigators work for the public and are not considered under the aegis of any one federal organization. Thus, there is no organized set of rules in this profession. Government regulations and enforcement has always affected the manner by which private information can be obtained and disseminated. These rules and regulations greatly impact upon the method and scope of the investigator's ability to perform his or her job.

As a profession, we should establish our own standards to which we should aspire and by which we can realistically measure self-regulation.

The concepts and ideas espoused in this manual are merely guidelines. There is no authority that dictates they be followed. They are a compilation of standards and ethics already in existence in those states that do require licensing and those state, national and international organizations that have seen fit to enforce a code of ethics for their members. This compendium of materials is a compilation and synopsis of ideals by which a majority of licensed investigators in our country are already guided.

The American Bar Association has published two works that deal similarly with the subject of standards and ethics. *Model Rules of Professional Conduct*[1] and *Legal Ethics*[2] provide guidelines for members of the legal profession. This volume is based in part upon the format and concepts of both of these works. Investigators generally work for, and our work frequently parallels the work of, the legal community. It seems fitting that this *Code of Professional Conduct* should adopt from the legal community some of the tried-and-true standards of that profession.

Although the *Code of Professional Conduct* is patterned after the *Model Rules of Professional Conduct*, it should be acknowledged that members of the investigative community work with attorneys, but are not necessarily licensed to practice law. As investigators working in support of litigation, finding evidence to be used by the legal community and providing information upon which legal cases will be settled, we are cognizant of the need to understand the accepted methods of our attorney-clients. We are, however, distinctively different. We work within the law as adjuncts, in many cases working for a member of the Bar. In these matters we assist in preparation for litigation, arbitration or mediation. There are times that our work is not used for adjudication. We are often hired merely for the information and knowledge necessary for the public to make informed decisions; be they corporations, private individuals or other entities.

On August 27, 1908 the American Bar Association approved thirty-two *Canons of Professional Ethics*. This code became the first such national code of accepted and expected conduct for the legal profession. Over the years, ethical opinions have guided, molded and modified the original canons. Like the *Canons of Professional Ethics* and the subsequent American Bar Association *Model Rules of Professional Conduct*, this compendium of ethical considerations has various subtexts, which further explain and amplify its meanings.

The following pages propose a code of ethics for the investigative community, based upon the rules and guidelines already present, adopted and practiced by many investigators. Changing times dictate the need to both modify and expand the basic ideals of this code. This is a flexible code of ethical behavior written as a guide by which our vocation may flourish. It is not intended to be static. Ethics are not dictates that can be carved in stone. New precedents, changes in social mores, and legislation will vary with political influence, cultural climate and professional preference. It is intended that this be a guide for fairness and civility for the investigative community.

These are the ideals to which we should aspire if we are to provide the highest form of professional service to our clients. The world is constantly changing. International strife and internal unrest affect us all. The internet has both simplified and complicated our access to information. New technology allows surveillance techniques unknown a decade ago. Access to information changes almost daily. It is still possible to maintain courtesy and respect for clients and colleagues while performing the job of the investigator. The creation of this code was intended as a standard to guide and inspire the practitioner to a higher plateau of professionalism. It is an effort to raise the image and practice of the investigator to one that is cognizant of respect and decency for all persons.

Endnotes

1 American Bar Association Center for Professional Responsibility, *Model Rules of Professional Conduct*, ABA Publications (Chicago, IL) 2015.

2 Ronald D. Rotunda, *Legal Ethics, The Lawyer's Deskbook on Professional Responsibility*, 2002-2003, West Group Publications (St. Paul, MN) 2002.

Preamble and Scope

[1] An investigator is entrusted with the job of finding information and evidence for a client or employer. This search promotes the very structure upon which our country was founded. The professional investigator is of service to the public, hired to perform particular assignments for private clients as and when the need arises. Other investigators are often retained by individual law firms, companies or corporations as employees. The information compiled by the investigator in each venue provides knowledge to the client.

[2] An investigator is charged with the responsibility of providing honest and fair service to the public. Investigators should discharge their duties with consideration, diligence and thoroughness. The investigator's conduct should be above reproach, within the dictates of the law, and for adequate and appropriate compensation. Competent service is to be expected. Justified reporting and billing are to be anticipated.

[3] The investigator is a private citizen with no additional rights or privileges, except where allowed by law. Therefore, the investigator's work must be within the scope of the laws governing all citizens. In this rapidly changing society our laws are malleable. They change constantly. The investigator is charged with being informed about those shifts in the law that impact upon their work. S/he should make a reasonable effort to understand these changes and respect the current law. An investigator may have the additional burden of responsibility to a licensing agency or authority within a particular venue that allows him or her the privilege of conducting the business of investigation.

[4] As a citizen, the investigator seeks improvement in the law for the benefit of the public and the profession. The investigator should be mindful of the importance of the vocation, making its services and purposes known, whenever possible.

[5] Prescribed laws dictate the conduct of an investigator. The investigator should adhere to principles of personal morality, ethics and fairness as an adjunct to these laws. This code is designed to assist the investigator in understanding the manner in which he or she can be expected to conduct business with respect to the public, the client and members of the profession.

[6] Investigators play a vital role in the preservation of society. The investigator assists private citizens with problems outside of the scope of law enforcement. An investigator's work helps to sustain peace of mind. The results of an investigator's findings often enable citizens to make decisions with dignity and sufficiency. The rules of professional conduct, when properly applied, define the relationship of the investigator to the society within which he or she functions. That society is composed of the legal system that dictates methods and procedures, the attorneys and clients with whom the investigator works, and private citizens and corporations who retain the services of professional investigators. Each of these societal segments presents the investigator with a wide variety of challenges to be addressed, researched and solved.

[7] This code is one of reason. It generally uses the term "should" instead of "must," given that there is no disciplinary authority to whom all investigators are responsible. The term "must" is only used when there are obligations under the law that dictate behavior for all investigators. There is nothing obligatory, as enforcement is not a consideration. Rather, these are definitions of conduct

dictated by civility, honor, honesty and good business practices. They are not "written in stone."

[8] Violation of a rule should not presuppose that a legal obligation has been breached. The rules are established as a guide to provide a foundation upon which investigators can structure their activity, and anticipate the conduct of others in the profession.

[9] Each rule is accompanied by a section entitled "Comment," proposed to further explain and illustrate its meaning. This "Preamble and Scope" is designed to be a general orientation to the context of the following chapters.

[10] Each rule is explained by a section entitled "Clarification," to explain each rule by example and specific instruction.

Summary of the Rules of Professional Conduct

Maintaining the Integrity of the Profession

Rule 1:1 Licensing

Proper registration and approval by applicable licensing authorities should be met before one seeks to initiate work in the field of professional investigation.

Rule 1:2 Certification

The investigator must not use credentials that do not apply and have not been earned and maintained.

Rule 1:3 Highest professional standards

To sufficiently serve the public, the investigator should maintain the highest professional standards. All investigations are to be conducted with integrity, honesty and excellence.

Rule 1:4 Abiding by the law

The investigator must, at all times, adhere to those legislated rules and regulations that apply to all other citizens.

Rule 1:5 Cooperation with law enforcement

An investigator should cooperate with all recognized and responsible law enforcement and governmental agencies, not interfering with ongoing investigations or knowingly promoting criminal activity.

Rule 1:6 Advertising and the investigator

Advertising of services by the investigator should be truthful, tasteful, and in compliance with the laws of the state in which he or she is licensed.

Rule 1:7 Solicitation for attorneys

An investigator should not solicit clients on behalf of an attorney or attorneys.

Rule 1:8 Misconduct

Investigators should not engage in professional misconduct, or fail to report the misconduct of others. Professional misconduct extends to criminal acts, falsification of information or violation of the *Code of Professional Conduct*.

<u>Investigator-Client Relations</u>

Rule 2:1 Scope of employment

The investigator works at the will of others. The services to be provided and the rules of engagement should be defined before beginning any work.

Rule 2:2 Competence

An investigator shall provide competent service for a client.

Rule 2:3 Diligence

An investigator shall act promptly and with reasonable diligence for all clients.

Rule 2:4 Communication

An investigator should keep a client reasonably informed.

Rule 2:5 Fees

All fees should be reasonable. Fees should be mutually agreed upon before beginning work and should be adequately explained to the client.

Rule 2:6 Confidentiality

Discretion and confidentiality by an investigator are expected and anticipated.

Rule 2:7 Conflict of interest
An investigator should not work for a client if that employment jeopardizes an investigation for another client.

Rule 2:8 Truthfulness and accuracy
It is incumbent upon the investigator to be truthful and accurate in advertising, in dealings with clients, in reporting findings, and in communications to any tribunal, court or law enforcement agency.

Rule 2:9 To do no harm
The investigator should be constantly mindful of the welfare of others, taking care to not knowingly do harm to any person.

Rule 2:10 Courtesy to the client and to the public
Courtesy and civility are to be extended to all clients and to the public.

Rule 2:11 Personal bias
Personal prejudice, bias, and political or religious beliefs should not be permitted to interfere with the faithful and honest discharge of an investigator's duty.

Rule 2:12 Records maintenance
The client's property should be preserved separately and safely, apart from other property in the investigator's possession. Investigators should maintain a system of record keeping that allows information to be retrieved for a reasonable time after the work has been completed.

Rule 2:13 Terminating a working relationship
An investigator's service for a client shall cease when either party has withdrawn from the working relationship and has clearly

informed the other that all work should be terminated. The relationship may be terminated by either the investigator or the client.

Investigator-Investigator Relations

Rule 3:1 Responsibilities of an investigator, agency owner, or license qualifier

The investigator must make reasonable efforts to ensure that all persons working with or for him or her adhere to the same rules and abide by the law in the same manner as the investigator.

Rule 3:2 Partner, employee or subcontractor responsibilities

All individuals working with or for an investigator are expected to adhere to the same rules of conduct demanded of the investigator.

Rule 3:3 Subcontractor regulations

A subcontractor is forbidden to contact the primary client directly unless authorized by the contracting firm.

Rule 3:4 Reputation of other investigators

An investigator will not directly or indirectly inhibit the future prospects or adversely affect the practice of another investigator.

Rule 3:5 Payment of work by other investigators

Investigators should compensate each other appropriately and expediently for work performed.

Rule 3:6 Multiple investigators working in concert

Responsibilities and reimbursement of each investigator should be clarified and confirmed before beginning an assignment. Responsibility and credit should be shared with all parties.

Rule 3:7 Competition between investigators

An investigator should not interfere with business contracts between other investigators and their clients.

Rule 3:8 Assistance and guidance between and for investigators

Assistance and guidance should be offered to investigators with lesser experience or those in need of help to complete an assignment. Education in the form of mentoring raises the level of knowledge and competency of all investigators.

<u>Transactions with Other Persons</u>

Rule 4:1 Respect for rights of third persons

The legal rights of all persons are to be respected by the investigator in the pursuit of evidence and information for a client. This includes the right to privacy and from harassment. Changing laws regarding privacy should be understood and respected.

Rule 4:2 Communication with persons represented by counsel

An investigator working for an attorney or a client who is represented by counsel is precluded from contacting an individual represented by opposing counsel. An investigator should not violate any rules regarding ex parte contact during an investigation. Internet and social media contact are herein included. It is the responsibility of the investigator not to overstep the limits implicit in ever-changing laws.

Rule 4:3 Communication with witnesses and persons being interviewed

All persons with whom an investigator must communicate regarding a matter under investigation are to be afforded all rights and privileges of any citizen. An investigator should respect and not infringe upon the rights of any person.

Rule 4:4 Communication regarding investigative services
An investigator should truthfully and accurately represent his or her services to the public. Investigative services and the investigator's abilities should be honestly portrayed.

The Code of
Professional Conduct

Maintaining the Integrity of the Profession

Rule 1:1 Licensing

Proper registration and approval by applicable licensing authorities should be met before one seeks to initiate work in the field of professional investigation.[1]

Comment

Regulations exist in most states governing the ability of an individual to practice the profession of private investigation. Multitudes of different licensing authorities regulate the investigator's work. A rule of law is established in those states that have licensing elaborating upon the extent and abilities of an investigator. Also, federal, state and local laws dictate the methods by which an investigator or an investigative agency must register to conduct a business and pay applicable taxes. It is incumbent upon the individual seeking to be a part of the investigative profession to determine which laws, statutes, rules and regulations apply and to uphold them to the fullest. An investigator should stay abreast of changes in laws governing his or her ability to engage in the business of investigation.

Clarification
[1] Appropriate licensing

> (a) An investigator should be appropriately licensed by the state, county or province within which she or he works, if such licensing is required. It is incumbent upon the investigator to seek out that authority, apply and qualify for any license issued.

(b) The investigator must abide by the laws in place that dictate behavior and ability to practice within a particular venue. Regulations governing investigators change from state to state. The investigator is charged with the responsibility of determining the particular laws affecting work in each jurisdiction in which he or she seeks to conduct business. The investigator should maintain knowledge of current changes in these laws.

(c) The investigator must pay all fees, taxes and levies that are required for an individual working within the jurisdiction of those applicable laws. The licensing authority may impose fees. Generally, federal, state and local taxes must be paid to conduct a business or to report income. All regulations applicable to businesses in general also apply to the investigator.

(d) If insurance and bonds are required of the investigator, then they must be obtained before beginning work. They must be maintained for the duration of any work within the jurisdiction. The need for posting a bond is a state-specific regulation and should be investigated and adhered to for the duration of work. Insurance is generally an optional requirement. General liability insurance and errors and omissions insurance is recommended to protect both the investigator and his or her clients. Workers' compensation insurance is not an option; it is required by law.

[2] States without licensing

(a) If licensing is not required, then the investigator must adhere to the laws, licenses and requirements for doing business in the jurisdiction.

(b) The investigator must register appropriately as a business entity, filing all requisite documents allowing one to establish a business, advertise and practice.

(c) The investigator must pay all fees, taxes and levies that are required for an individual working within the jurisdiction of those applicable laws.

[3] "In-House" investigators

(a) In some jurisdictions, investigators work "in-house" for law firms, insurance companies, corporations or other entities whose need for continued and repeated investigative services is constant.

(b) In some states (as of this writing) an investigator with only one employer is not required to be licensed. Investigators working for insurance companies as their primary employers may not fall into the category of those who are required to have a license or be regulated by a state authority.

(c) In such cases, the investigator should determine if any form of licensing is required by state or local statute before engaging in the profession.

Rule 1:2 Certification

The investigator must not use credentials that do not apply and have not been earned and maintained.

<u>Comment</u>

Various qualifying entities certify the skills of investigators. The profession is ancient, but the educational resources available to learn the craft other than through apprenticeship, have not been widely available until the middle of the twentieth century. Many national organizations offer certification attesting to the individual's achievement of a standard of proficiency in the field as a whole or within a particular discipline.[2] Universities, colleges, trade schools, internet courses and private institutions also offer certificates and degrees. The Investigator is cautioned to verify the value and quality of each course offered and its ability to aid in the ultimate goal of licensing in a particular state.

<u>Clarification</u>
[1] Credentials, certification and education

(a) An investigator must earn and maintain any credentials by fulfilling the requirements of the organization or entity that issues such certification. The qualifications of each certifying association or organization vary greatly. The investigator is charged with the responsibility of determining the requirements, making applications and qualifying for each individual certification sought. Once these qualifications have been attained either by testing or compliance, they must be maintained according to the dictates of each certifying authority.

(b) Continuing education may be required to maintain such certification. Those specific requirements must be met and appropriate dues paid if the investigator is to advertise his or her services under the auspices of this title. Continuing education credits are generally made available through attendance at educational seminars, publishing, or instructing others in a particular investigative skill. These credits toward preserving one's certification should be known and adhered to by the investigator wishing to maintain his or her credentials.

(c) No investigator should use a title that she or he has not earned or falsify credentials that mislead or misrepresent that investigator's abilities or qualifications.

[2] Misrepresentation or exaggeration of credentials

(a) The investigator must not misrepresent or exaggerate his or her abilities. An investigator should not take credit for having achieved a particular certification or for having attained a specific notoriety if that achievement were not truly accomplished. Misleading the public by exaggeration of skills and abilities places the public in jeopardy. Using unearned certification might result in depriving a more qualified investigator of the ability to perform a particular assignment or work for a client. It jeopardizes both the proper completion of the assignment and the reputation of the profession. Furthermore, it unfairly ascribes an appearance of competence to an individual who does not live up to the requirements of such anticipated ability.

(b) An investigator should accurately represent the education, training and experience he or she has achieved relevant to the profession. The investigator must represent to the client only those abilities, skills and achievements that were actually earned. Truthfulness in representation is a must.

(c) A curriculum vitae or resume should never contain false or misleading information. Nor should an investigator advertise his or her abilities in a particular discipline if that ability has not been acquired by experience or verified by a testing authority.

(d) An investigator should refrain from using any credentials that are false and misleading. These include falsification of education, accomplishments or work performed in an effort to entice a client or solicit work.

Rule 1:3 Highest Professional Standards

To sufficiently serve the public, the investigator should maintain the highest professional standards. All investigations are to be conducted with integrity, honesty and excellence.

Comment

The reputation of the entire industry often hinges on the activities of a single individual. Across-the-board adherence to the highest level of conduct is the only assurance that the profession will attain a position of respect within the communities where investigators function. All assignments should be completed with diligence. The investigative profession has suffered from notoriety based upon popular fiction. The false stereotypes of the television, cinema or fiction novel detective are an impediment to the reputation of the professional investigator. The result necessitates a high level of conduct by all investigators to counteract any stereotypes or untrue images.

Clarification

[1] Highest professional conduct

(a) Nothing that would demean the dignity and honor of the profession should be considered becoming conduct or activity for an investigator.

(b) Retaining a personal degree of ethical conduct ensures the public of the best assistance at the fairest prices done in the most acceptable manner. This extends to the client, persons with whom the investigator interacts, law enforcement or governmental agencies and the public.

(c) The investigator should aspire to do no harm by employing standards and equipment that will not impair the good name, good will, health or well-being of the client or the public at large.

(d) Adhering to the *Code of Professional Conduct* allows the investigator to live up to the standards necessary to provide the highest professional service.

[2] Business practices

(a) The investigator's business practices should not discredit the profession or any professional organization or association.

(b) Good business practices extend to the manner in which an investigator interacts with his or her employees, co-workers and other investigators. The investigator should strive for prompt completion of assignments, timely reporting, accurate information and punctual remuneration of debt.

(c) Maintaining accurate records, truthfully reporting findings and properly preserving evidence are also part of the good business practices of an investigator.

(d) Ethical conduct should be considered in regard to advertising and solicitation of clients. Presenting a truthful and accurate image is necessary to provide the client with sufficient information upon which to base a working relationship with the investigator.

(e) Adhering to federal, state and local laws regarding registrations, taxes and fees is the duty of every private citizen. It is no less for the investigator.

[3] Promote beneficial education and legislation

    (a) The investigator should promote programs designed to raise the standards of the profession. Concern for educating all investigators is the responsibility of each investigator. Continuing education programs and seminars provide information on proper procedures, state-of-the-art information, techniques and appropriate methods of conducting the business of the investigator.

    (b) Education programs designed to raise the level of knowledge and skill of all investigators are to be encouraged and supported. Attending such seminars and programs informs the investigator about progress within the industry, new and approved methods of conducting business and advanced techniques for finding evidence.

    (c) Legislation that is beneficial to the public interest should be supported. Legislation that enables investigators to access information and furthers work that benefits the public should be pursued. The investigator requires the ability to search and find evidence to support litigation, prevent fraud, discover the perpetrators of violence, locate and identify witnesses and nonpaying debtors and protect the rights of the public. In furtherance of these goals, the investigator should be constantly aware of legislation and support the enactment of new laws that are beneficial to the industry as a whole.

    (d) The investigator should always obey the law, taking care to uphold the rights and privileges afforded by the Constitution of the United States. The investigator should always consider the safety, health and well-being of the public when supporting legislation.

(e) As local, state and federal legislation change to adapt to newly invented technology concerns, the investigator is burdened with the responsibility of being reasonably familiar with laws impacting upon their work. The investigator is not necessarily an attorney and cannot be held to the same standard of knowledge. Reasonable effort, however, should be made to become familiar with those decisions and laws that affect the investigator's ability to legally perform his or her work.

(f) State legislators regularly amend the right of investigators to obtain specific information, such as access to state records. It behooves the investigator to be constantly mindful of changes in a given jurisdiction as what was available previously might not be still legally obtainable. Conversely, what was never before accessible to the investigator is potentially now available. It is the investigator's duty to be aware of these constant changes to the law.

[4] Personal demeanor

(a) The investigator should maintain a personal life consistent with his or her professional ethics.

(b) It behooves all investigators to adhere to a high level of personal moral and ethical behavior.

Rule 1:4 Abiding by the Law

The investigator must, at all times, adhere to those legislated rules and regulations that apply to all other citizens.

Comment

An investigator is a private citizen, not a law enforcement officer. Unless prescribed by law or allowed by legal exemption, the investigator has no authority or ability to ignore the law. The laws of our federal, state or local government, which apply to all citizens, apply equally to the private investigator.

Clarification

[1] Rights of the investigator

(a) The investigator has no extended rights or authority above or beyond that of any other private citizen. The investigator should conduct his or her business mindful of the responsibilities, rights and privileges of all citizens.

(b) The investigator is not a member of law enforcement and does not have a superior right to perform any act that is not legislated and approved by the dictates of law.

(c) Neither is the investigator inferior to any citizen. The investigator deserves the same consideration given to other members of the public and should not be treated in a lesser manner by any individual, authority or tribunal.

(d) The investigator may be limited by law in instances where attorney/clients have caveats against them as a result of current decisions regarding privacy. As a member of a legal team the restrictions placed upon an attorney/client also transcend to the investigator.

[2] Exemptions

(a) Some exemptions in the law allow the investigator access to information not readily available to the general public.

(b) These exemptions exist to facilitate the investigator's pursuit of information for clients. Accommodation by certain branches of government, law enforcement and the judiciary facilitate the investigator's access to information.

(c) The investigator should always obtain information lawfully and use it responsibly. Changes in the law require investigators to stay informed of limitations on their ability to seek and find information and evidence.

(d) The investigator should use these exemptions in a truthful and honest manner, being cognizant to do no harm in the pursuit of an assignment.

[3] Investigators ability to find information

(a) The education, skills and craft honed by investigators enhance their ability to identify information needed by the general public. Clients retain investigators for their knowledge of the manner in which information and evidence can be obtained.

(b) An investigator's experience and skills provide a service to the public. The investigator assists the legal system by complying with the rules of evidence. The work of the investigator is multifaceted. Clients use information for satisfaction or to solve problems. The investigator often provides information or evidence not readily available to a member of the public (individual, corporation, company or entity).

(c) Investigators work for plaintiffs or defendants in pursuit of the interests of all citizens exercising their rights and freedoms under the law.

(d) An investigator's capability to find information is not a matter of authority or permission, but of superior competence, experience and persistence.

(e) The expansion of the internet and social media has prompted a constantly changing volume of constraints and restrictions. They are varied, in flux and complex. Investigators must be mindful of the rapidly changing rules, laws and ethical constraints that impact upon the investigators work. These restraints pertain to the appropriate and acceptable use of public and private information.[3]

Rule 1:5 Cooperation with Law Enforcement

An investigator should cooperate with all recognized and responsible law enforcement and governmental agencies, not interfering with ongoing investigations or knowingly promoting criminal activity.

Comment

Investigative work often enters into the realm of law enforcement or governmental agencies. Criminal defense and civil litigation investigations may involve matters that are currently of concern to a branch of federal, state or local government.

Clarification

[1] Investigators should not impede ongoing investigations

(a) An investigator should never encroach upon any law enforcement or governmental agency's authority by knowingly taking action that impedes or interferes with an ongoing investigation. It is conceivable that an investigator's assignment might overlap with a matter that is concurrently of concern to a branch of law enforcement or government inquiry. Investigators should strive to avoid interfering with the work of any authoritative agency.

(b) Criminal defense investigations should be conducted without knowingly abetting the furtherance of criminal activity. The investigator should not promote or aid any criminal activity on the part of a client. Once an investigator discovers that his or her action has unwittingly promoted such activity, he or she should immediately withdraw from the assignment.

(c) An investigator should curtail surveillance or research that interferes with an investigation being concurrently performed by law enforcement or governmental agencies. It is conceivable that an investigation may unknowingly enter into the realm of an authoritative agency. When such action is discovered, the investigator should withdraw from any activity that would impede or infringe upon the work of that agency.

[2] Obstruction, deception or false statements

(a) An investigator should never obstruct justice, deceive, or give false statements to any law enforcement or government agency. Loyalty to the client should not extend to telling lies or giving false statements to an authoritative agency. The investigator's job is not to further criminal activity, but to discover evidence in support of a client's claim or defense.

(b) The investigator should not knowingly lie to law enforcement in the furtherance of his or her job. Rules of confidentiality, however, may prevent the investigator from revealing privileged data.

[3] Upholding the law

    (a) It is the duty of the investigator to respect and defend the freedoms, liberties, rights and privileges guaranteed to every citizen by the Constitution of the United States.

Rule 1:6 Advertising and the Investigator

Advertising of services by the investigator should be truthful, tasteful, and in compliance with the laws of the state in which he or she is licensed.

Comment

No investigator should falsify information relevant to education, ability or experience. Advertising should be done with every effort to promote a positive image for the entire profession. The investigator should avoid advertising that exaggerates his or her experience and abilities or discredits the investigative profession.

Clarification

[1] Truthfulness

    (a) Advertising should truthfully and accurately represent the services of an investigator. Investigative services and the investigator's ability should be honestly portrayed. Deception is inappropriate.

    (b) The investigator should only represent to the public information about his or her services that is accurate and correct. This extends to publications in all forms and media. It further includes word of mouth representation when speaking of abilities or accomplishments.

(c) The investigator should not claim ability or certification that has not been properly earned (see Rule 1:2, Certification). An investigator should not advertise credentials that were not earned or that are not current. Certification that has not been duly earned and awarded by the proper authority conveying such credential may not be displayed.

(d) Sufficient information should be provided to members of the public to make informed decisions about the use of investigative services and the particular investigator to employ. The public's expectations should not be unjustly raised by inaccurate or untrue advertising by an investigator. A client's financial investment should be contingent upon honest representation of credentials by the investigator.

[2] Improper advertising

(a) The investigator should never solicit to perform work that is illegal. The investigator should provide services and use methods that are allowable under law. She or he should never advertise to perform illegal services.

(b) The investigator should not induce or entice a member of the public to act in a matter that is criminal by advertising services he or she knows are not lawful. Obtaining information is the nature of investigative work. The investigator should not engage in or encourage the gathering of information through means that are criminal.

(c) It is inappropriate for an investigator to take credit for work that he or she has not performed. Falsification of information is misleading and unfair to the public. Claiming ability or exaggerating experience when it has not been duly earned discredits the profession and places the client in harm's way.

[3] Promoting a positive image

(a) Public misconceptions about the investigative profession have been created by popular fiction and mass media reporting. It is incumbent upon the investigator to promote the professionalism of the industry by eschewing trite and distasteful advertising. The investigator should not feed public misconceptions by promoting a negative image of the profession.

(b) An investigator should fully explain his or her services to educate the public about the nature and abilities of the professional. Misconceptions and stereotypes do a disservice to the practicing professional investigator. The investigator should help to dispel the myths by not falsifying or exaggerating his or her abilities.

Rule 1:7 Solicitation for Attorneys

An investigator should not solicit clients on behalf of an attorney or attorneys.

<u>Comment</u>

It is not the investigator's job to procure clients for attorneys. Referrals are appropriate in circumstances dictating a need and when an individual has requested such a referral from the investigator.

<u>Clarification</u>

[1] Acting as a "runner"[4]

(a) It is improper and inappropriate for an investigator to act as a "runner" for any attorney or law firm. Lawyers and law firms are precluded from employing "runners." It would therefore be unethical (and in some states criminal) for an investigator to act in such a capacity.

(b) Investigators are in the business of finding evidence about existing cases already the responsibility of an attorney or client. It is not the job of the investigator to create or manufacture cases for the attorney or client.

[2] Exceptions

(a) If a private client has retained an investigator to perform investigative work on a matter and is in need of legal counsel, it is appropriate for the investigator to recommend an attorney.

(b) If the client does not have legal representation but seeks legal advice, it is appropriate for an investigator to refer the matter to an attorney or law firm.

(c) The investigator is precluded from accepting fees from that attorney or law firm contingent upon the outcome of an investigation (see Rule 2:5, Fees).

Rule 1:8 Misconduct

Investigators should not engage in professional misconduct or fail to report the misconduct of others. Professional misconduct extends to criminal acts, falsification of information or violation of the *Code of Professional Conduct*.

Comment

Self-regulation is necessary within the profession of the

investigator to assure the highest degree of service to the public. Proper adherence to all laws is necessary for investigators to protect themselves, the client and public. Fraud and deceit through misrepresenting ability or service discredits the profession and harms the public. Using methods that are unscrupulous further discredits the individual investigator and the entire profession.

<u>Clarification</u>
[1] Violating the code

(a) Knowingly violating the *Code of Professional Conduct* or inducing or instructing others to do so is considered misconduct. The *Code of Professional Conduct* was conceived from ethical codes previously established to regulate the activities of investigators for the betterment of the profession and the public. Intentional violation of these tenets demeans the individual investigator and the profession as a whole.

(b) The moral considerations of the code reflect the investigator's fitness for performing his or her job. Conduct not governed by law may affect that fitness. The principles of the code are intended to uphold the highest level of professional conduct for all investigators. These ideals cannot necessarily be legislated, but they ensure quality service to the public and a heightened level of professionalism for the investigator.

(c) Any conduct that compromises the investigator's ability to provide honest, trustworthy and legal service to the public should be considered misconduct. The investigator should do nothing that hinders the administration of justice or the rights and privileges afforded by the constitution.

[2] Violating the law
(a) The investigator must not knowingly engage in criminal

action in the course of his or her work. Investigators must uphold the law and work within its limitations.

(b) Investigators concerned about existing laws that unintentionally hinder the progress of an investigation should work within the proper system to change those laws. Violating a law is not an appropriate method of displaying dissatisfaction. Proper channels of the legal system should be used to seek appropriate changes through legislation favorable to the investigator and the public they serve.

(c) The investigator should never suggest or counsel any person to act in violation of the law or to commit any criminal act. It is not, however, criminal to discuss the law and its ramifications upon an investigation. Such counseling or discussion should be done to educate all persons who may hold misconceptions about the limits of an investigator's abilities.

(d) The law is an organic discipline which changes regularly. A professional investigator has a responsibility to be reasonably acquainted with those decisions in law and in ethics that impact upon the performance of his or her duties.

(e) The investigator is not necessarily a lawyer. He or she would be advised to take reasonable measures or seek legal advice if questions arise regarding acceptable procedures.

Investigator-Client Relations

Rule 2:1 Scope of Employment

The investigator works at the will of others. The services to be provided and the rules of engagement should be defined before beginning any work.

Comment

In the private sector, the investigator's role is that of a service provider, working either for an employer or individual client in need of assistance. The investigator should know what is expected of him or her and should explain the extent of work performed and the type of information that can reasonably be obtained. The investigator is not a servant to blindly obey the demands of any client. He or she has a responsibility to only perform work that is legally responsible and morally defensible. A client's wish is not an investigator's obligation.

Clarification

[1] Fully explain to the client

(a) It is incumbent upon the investigator to fully explain the spectrum of possible options open to a client in need of services. This includes a complete explanation of the investigator's credentials, methods of operation and fees. Various methods of work may be presented for consideration. The nature and scope of work performed by an investigator should be explained to educate the client.

(b) The client should be apprised of the variety of techniques used and diversity of information that is legally obtainable by the investigator. The client may hold misconceptions about the procedures by which information is legally obtained. These misunderstandings or false expectations should be corrected. It is not unusual for a client to have unrealistic hopes about the investigator's job based upon stereotypes found in popular fiction. The investigator should clarify the methods and manner of work for the benefit of the client.

(c) The client has the ultimate authority to determine the purposes of the investigation and to direct the investigator toward those ends. The client is financially responsible for the work. He or she (or the company or entity that he or she represents) should have direct input into the goals toward which an investigation should proceed. Furthermore, the client retains the authority to direct the investigation toward preferred goals and information.

(d) The client and the investigator should mutually agree on a course of action to be taken by the investigator. The client's preferences should not discount the ability and knowledge of the investigator. Both parties should mutually agree upon the decisions so that the client and the investigator share the same goal.

(e) The investigator should abide by the client's decisions, so long as they are not grounded in unethical or illegal activity. The investigator should inform the client if his or her desires for performance are criminal in nature. Any conduct, civil or criminal, that jeopardizes the rights of another or places the investigator in a position of supporting inappropriate conduct should be discussed with the client. The investigator should never engage in any activity that is illegal for the furtherance of a client's desires for information. The investigator has a duty to discuss alternative methods of work that are within the law.

(f) The investigator has no obligation to pursue objectives or perform duties simply because a client wishes him or her to do so. The investigator is not a servant under the client's direction. The investigator should not knowingly act in any manner that is inappropriate or criminal in an effort to please the client. The investigator is a highly professional service provider. The investigator is not to follow the orders of a client if they are adverse to the investigator's moral or professional precepts.

(g) The investigator's representation of a client does not constitute an endorsement of the client's political, economic, social or moral views or activities.

[2] Not condone criminal activity

(a) An investigator should not condone illegal action. There is no obligation for an investigator to act in a manner that is criminal.

(b) An investigator should counsel clients against illegal or unethical action. A client may be ignorant of the laws governing an investigator's actions. The investigator should educate the client on the extent of his or her ability under the law.

(c) The investigator should further inform the client of his or her own personal ethical constraints against such action. The investigator should withdraw from any work that is inconsistent with his or her own moral or ethical beliefs. So too should the investigator withdraw from performing in a manner that is criminal.

(d) The investigator should inform the client of the ramifications of any action of a questionable nature. Although the investigator may discuss such action with the client this is not an endorsement of illegal activity. This discussion should be used to educate and inform the client of the consequences of unlawful activity.

[3] Estimates of results, time and costs

(a) Anticipated results, expected time limits and financial costs should be explained to the client before beginning an assignment.

(b) The investigator should give the client a realistic assessment of the likelihood of obtaining information and evidence. The client should be given a general description of the type of information that is likely to result from an investigation.

(c) The investigator should make no promises about the results to be obtained. The investigator is not a fortune teller or seer. Results cannot always be anticipated. The client deserves a truthful assessment of all possible results and anticipated time schedules.

(d) Realistic time limits should be established in which to anticipate that an assignment will be completed. This is sometimes a difficult task, depending on the nature and scope of an assignment. In such cases the client should be apprised of this difficulty. At the very least, realistic time frames of communication should be established to allow the client the ability to make informed decisions

(e) Estimations of costs, methods of billing, fees and expenses should be discussed with the client before starting work. Retainer deposits, flat rates for work performed or hourly billing should all be discussed and agreed upon before any work is performed. (See Rule 2:5, Fees.) Because it is often difficult to predict the ultimate cost of an investigation, it is appropriate for the investigator to work for incremental payments so that the client has control over the amount of money spent on his or her behalf. Billing arrangements should be agreed to before any work is performed.

Rule 2:2 Competence

An investigator shall provide competent service for a client.

Comment

Competence requires the knowledge, skill, thoroughness and preparation reasonably necessary to provide adequate service.

Clarification

[1] Licensing

(a) Competence first starts with appropriate licensing, if available. No one national standard or uniform licensing is available to dictate the level of knowledge, skill or thoroughness to which an investigator must aspire. Licensing, as of this writing, is performed individually by each state under the auspices of various licensing authorities.

(b) If licensing is required, then the investigator must qualify for the specific regulations of the appropriate licensing authority. If multi-state or jurisdictional work is to be performed by an investigator, he or she must adhere to the dictates of each individual licensing authority, even if these regulations may differ (see Rule 1:1, Licensing).

[2] Necessary training

(a) An investigator need not necessarily have special training or prior experience to handle a problem new to the investigator.

(b) The investigation in question may be focused on a subject matter never before encountered by an investigator. The type of question encountered by the investigator need not be one previously investigated in the past. The investigator should not be excluded from accepting a wholly new type of assignment.

(c) Skills transcend knowledge. Proficiency and faculty developed through training and experience equip the investigator to work on cases never before encountered. Although the knowledge required may vary from case to case, the competent investigator has honed skills that are useful regardless of a case's subject matter. The diligent, determined and thorough investigator will use similar techniques and procedures to fulfill many different assignments. Different cases share common features and procedures. Experience in the subject matter of a case is not a prerequisite for a successful investigation.

(d) An investigator may provide adequate representation on a wholly novel subject matter through necessary preparation. Association with another investigator whose knowledge and experience makes him or her more accomplished may facilitate the process.

(e) Education and study of a new or unusual subject may be sufficient. Investigators have access to a wide variety of data regarding technique, method and resources through continuing education programs and the mentoring of others in the profession.

[3] Legal guidance

(a) If appropriate, an investigator should request that the client seek legal advice explaining and outlining those areas of evidence required to conduct an appropriate investigation.

(b) An investigator is capable of gathering evidence. An investigator is not necessarily an attorney. It is the attorney who should dictate what evidence is most appropriate to assist in the adjudication of a client's problems. An investigator should not provide legal advice to any client.

(c) If no attorney represents the interests of the client, then the investigator is charged with the responsibility of obtaining as much information and evidence available by due diligent searching within the financial limitations of the client. The client should be informed that this information is being gathered in the usual form and to the best abilities of the investigator, but does not necessarily constitute all the information and evidence that will be necessary to substantiate the client's claim or otherwise complete the assignment.

[4] Continuing education

(a) Competence necessitates that an investigator continually seek to improve his or her level of excellence by study. Reading professional literature, attending seminars or taking continuing educational programs advances the knowledge of the investigator. The persistent pursuit of information is vital.

(b) It is essential that each practitioner become familiar with new and changing legislation affecting the abilities of the investigator to function within our society. Knowledge of existing laws and participation in the process that creates new legislation enables the investigator to provide the best service to the public. The investigator must not knowingly act in a manner that is contrary to any law.

(c) Being fully apprised of changes in legislation enable the investigator to uphold the principles of the *Code of Professional Conduct*. An investigator should keep abreast of proposed legislation and be involved in the process that creates rules and regulations for the investigative professional. This can be accomplished by membership in associations dedicated to the monitoring and implementation of legislation affecting the investigative industry.[5]

(d) Investigators who specialize in particular areas of work should continually seek to increase their knowledge of those changes in technology and information influencing the value of the evidence. Criminal investigators, in particular, should understand the importance and effectiveness of advanced technology as it applies to their assigned cases.[6]

[5] Understanding the assignment

(a) Competent handling of a particular matter includes fully understanding the assignment, agreeing with the client or employer about the information or evidence sought, and diligently investigating to fulfill the assignment.

(b) Thoroughness, within the restrictions and confines of the financial limitations imposed by the client, is expected. The ability to completely exhaust all avenues of investigation may be limited by the client's inability to finance continued investigative work. An investigator can provide the most competent service by prioritizing tasks to best meet the needs of the client.

(c) Diligent pursuit of information through acceptable techniques and within the law is a necessity.

[6] Understanding one's own abilities

(a) It is incumbent upon the practicing professional to understand the scope and extent of his or her own abilities based upon education, experience and training before entering into a contractual relationship to perform investigative services.

(b) If the investigator's knowledge and abilities have not been tested by experience, it may benefit him or her to seek credentials through a certifying authority that can better judge qualifications.

(c) The investigator should understand his or her own capacity for accepting assignments based on current workload requirements. Time constraints imposed by existing clients should also be weighed when deciding whether to accept new work. Capability extends not only to knowledge and skills but to the time available to satisfy the client's need for information. Juggling too many responsibilities minimizes the investigator's effectiveness on all cases.

Rule 2:3 Diligence

An investigator shall act promptly and with reasonable diligence for all clients.

Comment

The investigator should make every effort within the bounds of the law and the financial limitations of the client in furtherance of the investigation.

Clarification

[1] Reasonable expectation of service

(a) A client has an expectation that services are being performed with the best efforts of the investigator in a timely manner.

(b) This expectation is reasonable and should be of primary concern to the investigator. An assignment should not be undertaken if the investigator doubts his or her capacity to properly complete the work because of experience, skill, constraints of finances or limitations of time. The investigator should not accept assignments that he or she cannot complete in a reasonable interval because of the demands of work for others.

(c) The investigator should pursue each matter on behalf of a client in spite of obstacles and opposition that might impede his or her progress. It is understood that the work is often difficult, requiring excessive hours in unpleasant circumstances. These inconveniences should not deter him or her. Assignments are sometimes seemingly impossible, but persistent pursuit of information by the investigator, despite obstacles, may prove successful in the end.

(d) Every effort should be made to satisfy an assignment, even when it is inconvenient, difficult or arduous.

[2] Professional discretion

(a) An investigator has professional discretion to determine the means by which a matter should be pursued.

(b) All matters contracted with a client should be pursued as promised. The investigator should not undertake an assignment that he or she cannot fulfill. The best efforts of the investigator should be expended to complete the work in a satisfactory manner.

[3] Timeliness of all assignments

(a) An investigator should not procrastinate in the execution of work to be performed for a client. The interests of the client should not be compromised or otherwise affected in a manner adverse to the client's interests by the passage of time.

(b) Timely representation may affect the value of information being provided. Court deadlines or personal requirements may require the search for information to be completed within a definite time. The investigator should endeavor to stay within the client's time limits so as to have no adverse effects.

(c) The client has an expectation of service within a reasonable period of time that should be respected by the investigator. A client's concept of a reasonable time, however, might differ from the investigator's. Communication should be maintained between parties to ensure that the necessary labors are being performed in a manner that is useful for the client.

[4] Completion of work

(a) All matters contracted for, or agreed to, as a part of an investigative assignment should be completed.

(b) However, when either the investigator or the client has severed a relationship before the job is completed, the case may go unfinished. In such cases, the termination should be done in accordance with the best interests of all parties. The product of the investigation at the time of termination should be preserved for future use by the client. (See Rule 2:13, Termination of work.)

(c) An exception would occur when the client's financial limitations prevent the client from sufficiently funding continued work by the investigator. An investigator is not expected to work without payment. Pro bono work for indigent clients is always encouraged as a means of ensuring that all persons have an opportunity to pursue their cases to satisfactory conclusions. It is not a requirement of the profession.

Rule 2:4 Communication

An investigator should keep a client reasonably informed.

Comment

The client's requests for information should be addressed and reasonable expectations for information should be fulfilled. He or she should be informed sufficiently to make decisions regarding the continued work of the investigator on his or her behalf.

Clarification

[1] Timely communication

(a) Regular communication is necessary so that the client may make informed decisions regarding the matter under investigation.

(b) The nature of investigation is such that information or evidence may not be readily available or easily obtainable. Information may or may not be available according to a client's desired schedule. The client should be informed of this possibility. The investigator should make every effort to work within the timetable necessary for the client.

(c) Evidence is not always available within an anticipated time frame. Frequently, long periods elapse during the course of investigative work in spite of the due diligence of the investigator. The investigator cannot be responsible for information or evidence that is not available on demand. The investigator should maintain communication with the client to explain such possibilities.

(d) The client should be continually and adequately informed of the progress of any investigation even if no new or additional evidence is gathered. It is not the responsibility of the investigator to create results. It is possible that, in the course of extended investigative work, no new or extraordinary findings will be made. The client should be informed of continued progress and effort even if new evidence has not been discovered.

(e) The client should be provided with results even when they are contrary to his or her desired outcome. Optimal results of an investigation cannot be dictated or preconceived. The investigative findings sometimes do not benefit the client.

In such cases, the client should be fully informed of this information because it affects the decision-making process.

[2] Information revealed to the client

    (a) Adequate communication does not require that all investigative strategy and resources should be revealed to the client.

    (b) Reasonable client expectations for information should be fulfilled. The client pays for the investigator's services. Therefore, the client has a right to understand the progress an investigator is making on his or her behalf. This does not presume that all methods and findings be revealed at all times. The client should anticipate a reasonable system of communication that allows the investigator to pursue the task at hand.

    (c) Often clients are unreasonable. Frequently a client's perception of the investigator's work is illogical. Expectations that the investigator should have access to privileged information and be capable of expedited work are sometimes irrational. Demands for such results should be dealt with by educating the client about the realities of the investigator's work.

    (d) The client should have sufficient information to make informed decisions about continued endeavors by the investigator. He or she deserves to understand the progress and anticipated conclusion of a matter under investigation. The client often has to make decisions that will affect his or her personal safety, schedule or plans. The investigator owes the client sufficient information to make such decisions in a responsible manner.

(e) Exact details of the investigator's techniques or sources of information need not be revealed.

[3] Client's capacity for information

(a) Communication is generally anticipated on a regular and ongoing basis with any client who is a comprehending and responsible adult.

(b) If the client is a child, mentally impaired, or otherwise unable to make informed decisions for him—or herself, the investigator need not impart all information to that individual. In such cases, a responsible party, guardian ad litem or attorney in fact should be used, if possible.

(c) If the client is an association or other organization, the investigator may not be able to adequately communicate with each individual. Communication through a designated agent is appropriate.

[4] Acting without authority of communication

(a) An investigator may act for a client without prior consultation in matters when it is impractical to do otherwise.

(b) In instances involving "hot pursuit" of information, the investigator may find it necessary to immediately follow a trail of information without first communicating with the client.

(c) Eventual communication at a reasonable time would be anticipated.

Rule 2:5 Fees

All fees should be reasonable. Fees should be mutually agreed upon before beginning work and should be adequately explained to the client.

Comment

Investigators should uphold and never abuse the principle of appropriate and adequate compensation. Fees should be agreed upon before an investigation. A report sufficient to justify expenditures should be provided at the conclusion of work. Several factors affecting the imposition of fees should be considered when they are established. Fees should be adequate to the assignment.

Clarification

[1] Criteria for fees

(a) Fees should be reasonable. Several criteria may be used to establish fees. The investigator should promote the concept of adequate payment for services rendered.

(b) Fees should be based upon time, labor and expenses. Billable hours do not always equate with time expended for a client. When establishing a fee schedule the investigator should consider all possible labor, expenditures of time, file preparation, review, evaluation, report writing, and expenses. The degree of difficulty of a task may also be factored into the final rates.

(c) Special skills necessary to pursue an assignment should be considered. Experience, reputation and ability in a particular area of expertise should be weighed. Advanced training, experience or education may make an investigator more qualified and able to provide a higher level of expertise. Fees may be adjusted to accommodate such superior service.

(d) The investigator should consider the likelihood that accepting an assignment will prevent him or her from performing other work or concurrently accepting new employment. The all-encompassing nature of an assignment may deter an investigator from simultaneously fulfilling work obligations for other clients. When one assignment infringes upon the time necessary to complete other work, appropriate adjustments may be made for compensation.

(e) Established fees may vary between territorial areas. Urban communities tend toward a higher norm than suburban or rural areas. The geographic location of available investigators may be limited, placing higher demand on those who are licensed to practice. The average fees prevailing in his or her area do not bind an investigator. An investigator should set his or her fees proportionate to the quality of work being performed, the effort and energy required and the degree of difficulty encountered. It is appropriate for an investigator to charge more or less than others in their geographic region.

(f) Expedited time constraints or emergency investigations may influence fees. Expectations of work to be performed within limited periods to meet a client's deadline or immediate needs are to be considered. Last minute or crisis assignments may be billed at a higher rate than assignments that could be performed at the leisure of the investigator. Working during holidays, overtime or to meet the deadlines of clients who have procrastinated may be compensated for by higher billing rates.

(g) Established relationships with a particular client may affect fees. A special rate charged may be considered for repetition and volume of work. Discounted services to repeat clientele do not do a disservice to the individual who hires the investigator infrequently.

(h) Fees may be charged per hour or per assignment. If mutually agreed upon by both parties, it is appropriate to set a per assignment or per diem rate. The investigator should consider all the ramifications of the work, time, inability to service other clients, difficulty, danger and effort before setting such fees. The client must agree upon these fees before work is performed.

(i) It is appropriate for an investigator to establish specific fees for depositions or court appearances. Rates may be greater than the normal hourly billing of the investigator because such appearances will preclude him or her from performing any other task. The time necessary for preparation, travel and perhaps lodging and food expenses may be included in these fees or may be separately invoiced.

(j) All investigators should promote the concept of adequate compensation for work performed.

[2] Contingency Fees

(a) An investigator is not allowed to charge on a contingency-fee basis when the outcome of an investigation might be slanted, tainted or prejudiced because of financial incentive.

(b) The success or failure of the matter under investigation shall in no way affect the amount of payment to the investigator.

There should be no financial incentive that would prejudice an investigation in any manner.

(c) Investigators are truth seekers not case makers. The outcome of a particular investigation cannot be preordained. The very nature of investigative work is to discover information or evidence that has not as yet been identified.

(d) An investigator should not be financially induced toward a particular result.

(e) Instances where contingency fees would be acceptable include assignments where there is no adversarial party conflict, and thus no opportunity for prejudicing the outcome of an investigation. Incentive pay in the form of contingency payment for expedited work in locating a person, commodity or asset would be acceptable (i.e. finding a witness, locating missing assets in an estate, recovering missing or stolen artwork).

(f) No one should be deprived of his or her rights as a result of an investigator's personal benefit through contingency fee agreements. In fact, many states have laws precluding fee sharing between investigators and attorneys to prevent such inequities.

[3] Bribes, gratuities and commissions

(a) An investigator must never accept a bribe, gratuity or commission that would be an incentive for prejudicing the quality or results of an investigation.

(b) An investigator's work is to find the information, evidence and facts that truly exist. Having predisposed results biased toward a particular end is contrary to the investigator's job.

(c) Any bribe or gratuity that would influence an investigator to slant or bias an investigation is unethical. Financial payment, promise of reward or remuneration of any kind that would direct a conclusion other than that which is actually found in fact should not be accepted.

(d) An investigator must not direct an investigation toward a predisposed end. Rather, an investigator must follow the path to which real evidence and the facts will lead.

[4] Written compensation agreements

(a) A writing is the best method of insuring agreement of all parties. Terms of compensation should be explained and agreed upon before work is begun for any client. An investigator may charge hourly, daily or per case rates. The client should be aware of the basis upon which compensation is being computed. It is not necessary to explain all factors underlying the investigator's decision to bill in a particular manner. The method, manner and rates of compensation should be put in writing.

(b) Compensation should be mutually agreed upon before beginning work. It is suggested that written agreements be completed to protect the investigator and the client in the event of a dispute.

(c) In an effort to avoid fee disputes with a client after the beginning of an investigation, it is recommended that an investigator use a fee agreement. Such an agreement can be included as part of a contract for services.

(d) A fee agreement need not be in writing. Fee agreements

should, however, be thoroughly discussed and agreed upon by all parties before work is started. A written agreement makes later misinterpretation less likely, but does not negate the possibility of a dispute at a later time.

[5] Retainer deposits

(a) It is considered to be a good business practice and acceptable for the investigator to request and accept a retainer deposit. A retainer deposit is a form of insurance covering time expended, expenses paid and ancillary costs. A deposit protects the investigator against nonpayment by clients who may be unhappy with the results of an investigation.

(b) Unused portions of any retainer are to be returned to the client unless otherwise stipulated and agreed upon. The exception to this would occur when a per diem or per assignment fee has been charged and payment has been made in advance of the job's performance.

(c) The investigator is performing a service. The product is released when the results of an investigation are revealed to the client. It is acceptable for an investigator to request payment in advance to ensure that compensation is received for work performed.

(d) A client may not be satisfied with the results of an investigation if these results are not the product desired. He or she may not respect the investigator's efforts or consider that the investigator has worked the case, performed investigative tasks and incurred expenses on the client's behalf.

(e) The investigator is responsible for pursuing the

investigation diligently but is not responsible for the actual findings of the investigation. Payment is expected based upon this premise.

[6] Accounting

(a) Investigators should provide for fair and accurate accounting of all charges agreed upon.

(b) An investigator should explain his or her method of billing, the items to be charged, and the manner in which invoices will be presented. A procedure should be spelled out and agreed upon in advance between client and investigator.

(c) Invoices should account for hours expended and expenses incurred in furtherance of the client's investigation.

(d) It is acceptable to charge "per case" or "per diem." Invoices in such cases need not be itemized.

[7] Exceptions

(a) Changes to agreed-upon charges are only acceptable when they are necessary to preserve life, property or evidence.

(b) When an assignment is terminated by either the investigator or the client, all further expenditures should cease. A possible exception would include accumulation of fees for additional effort in preparation of a final report and accounting.

(c) Another exception occurs when information has been requested or services of subcontractors have been retained but the results not yet received by the investigator at the time of the termination. In such cases, payment for that anticipated work product may be included as a part of the final billing.

Rule 2:6 Confidentiality

Discretion and confidentiality are expected of an investigator.

Comment

An investigator should not reveal information obtained from the client or learned during the course of investigation to anyone except the client contracting for that information. The investigator is dealing with private or privileged information and must respect the client's confidences. There are exceptions when information may be revealed.

Clarification

[1] Client confidentiality

(a) The investigator is expected to maintain confidentiality regarding all information learned from the client. She or he may be privy to information revealed by the client during the employment. All information that the client reveals, either as background to an investigation or as a result of exchange of information, is not intended or authorized to be made known to any other individual or entity.

(b) Nothing learned by the investigator about the client or the client's case is information for any party other than the client. An exception can occur if it is relevant or necessary to further investigative work and is revealed with the knowledge of the client.

(c) Information about the client or the substance of a case may necessarily be revealed during the course of an investigation to advance the process of gathering information and evidence. The client should be aware and agree to the use of certain amounts of information being made public.

[2] Case confidentiality

(a) Confidentiality is expected of the investigator with respect to all information obtained during the course of his or her work for the client. It is not uncommon for members of the public to be interested in the work of the investigator. The investigator, however, has a duty not to discuss the specifics of a matter if that discussion will lead to a breach of confidentiality.

(b) Information obtained for the client is intended solely for the client. The materials and intelligence gathered are done for the purpose of furthering the client's case. This information is a part of the case file and not to be disseminated in any form to any unauthorized party.

(c) No information learned or obtained during an investigation should be revealed to any individual without the client's express permission. This extends to the attorney representing the client, unless the attorney is a named client in the assignment. The investigator should obtain permission from the client before sharing information with the client's attorney. Discussions about the client with the attorney are to be limited to those areas previously approved.

[3] Confidentiality of records

(a) Confidentiality extends to the manner in which all records are maintained, disseminated and destroyed.

(b) Client files, including the confidential information therein, are to be maintained in a manner that promotes the highest level of security and privacy. Filing and computer systems containing client information should be made secure from any individual not working on the particular investigation within an investigator's office.

(c) Individuals not working on or directly involved in the investigative process for the client (investigators and adjutant staff in the investigator's office) have no right or reason to view any proprietary information contained therein.

(d) Computer security, the storage of computer-based information, leaves open the possibility of intrusion or hacking[7] by non authorized persons. Every effort should be made and regularly revisited to ensure that storage methods are secure from destruction or deletion (either inadvertent or intentional.) Files and proprietary information should be kept private from unauthorized persons. Periodic safeguards, password changes, firewalls and upgrades should be a part of the investigators standard practice and procedure.

(e) Reports created for the client are the client's property. They are not to be provided to any individual other than the person who has contracted for the work being performed. File information may not be shared in cases of multiparty litigation without first obtaining permission from the client to make revelations.

(f) Disposal of file information should be conducted so as to ensure the continued privacy of the client (see Rule 2:12 Records Maintenance).

[4] Confidentiality builds trust

(a) Confidentiality encourages the client toward candor and honesty when dealing with investigators. Trust can and should be established so the client feels comfortable revealing intimate details without embarrassment or fear of consequence. The investigator has to learn and understand all relevant information as a basis upon which to build an investigation. This can only be accomplished when the client can trust the investigator.

(b) Withholding vital data can affect the investigator's ability to perform his or her job effectively or efficiently. The discomfort of a client who exhibits a lack of confidence in the investigator may result in information being withheld. It is vital to place the client in a position of trust wherein all necessary information will be passed on to the investigator in furtherance of the investigation.

(c) The client should be informed that complete disclosure of all facts by the client avoids the investigator's need to develop information already known. This prevents a financial burden to the client and facilitates the work of the investigator.

[5] Exception: litigation and subpoenas

(a) There is an implied authorization to disclose information to the extent necessary to carry out the requirements of an assignment.

(b) When evidence has been gathered for a client in support of litigation, it may be necessary for the investigator to make revelations about or from the case file that are necessary to comply with the rules of court.

(c) Information and evidence may enter the public domain as a result of depositions, court appearances or subpoenas. In such cases the investigator is bound by the rules of court. The investigator should understand the concept of attorney work-product privilege and discuss with client and clients counsel the value of being retained directly by the attorney in preservation of evidence.

(d) Attorney work product privilege is not necessarily a bar against requests for investigators files. Current law and precedential cases are constantly changing. When served with either an official or casual request for files or file contents an investigator would be well served to notify appropriate counsel to bear the burden of protecting privileged information and client strategies from being shared with adverse counsel.[8]

(e) If served with a subpoena, the investigator should immediately contact the client or client's legal counsel. Legal procedures may be employed to render that process service invalid or ineffective. It may be advisable for the investigator to seek personal counsel at this time, if clients counsel is not sufficiently helpful.

[6] Exception: criminal activity

(a) An exception is noted when the breach of confidentiality is necessary to prevent the client from committing a criminal act that the investigator believes may result in death or severe bodily harm.

(b) An investigator cannot assist or advise a client in furtherance of a criminal act. If the likelihood of such assistance or advice is imminent as a result of continued work with and for the client, then the investigator should cease to work with that client.

[7] Exception: establishing a claim

(a) An exception is noted when the breach of confidentiality is necessary for an investigator who must establish a claim or defense to protect himself or herself in a court of law.

(b) It may become necessary for an investigator to build a defense to a charge by a client or to counter a claim in which the client was involved. Information known to the investigator would then be revealed.

(c) During a dispute in which a client makes accusations about an investigator, file information may be revealed to protect the investigator from spurious action, costly litigation or publicity that would impugn his or her reputation.

[8] Media and publication

(a) An investigator must consider the consequences of discussing any case with the media (television, news media and other journalistic endeavors) at any time. The investigator may not use his or her involvement in an investigation as an advertisement or solicitation without permission from the client to do so. Successfully completed work for a client is not automatically an endorsement of the investigator's services and should not be used as such.

(b) An investigator should refrain from divulging information to the media that would jeopardize a client's case. It is not his or her role to reveal privileged information that might adversely affect the trial strategy of an attorney working for the client.

(c) With the exception of a court action, the matter is governed under the rules of confidentiality (see Rule 2:6, Confidentiality).

(d) During a court action, the investigator must be concerned with his or her ability to influence a jury or tribunal by discussing matters pertinent to the case at hand. An investigator participating in an investigation shall not make public statements that may materially prejudice adjudicative proceedings.

(e) Investigators are frequently called upon for interviews by the press to discuss their work in general. In such cases, specific instances that might reveal the name or nature of confidential employment should not be cited. Generalities that do not specifically identify or allude to the identity of a client or a client's problem are acceptable. It is permissible to discuss a case with the client's authorization.

(f) The investigator should, at all times, be cognizant that his or her desire for public recognition must be secondary to the greater needs of the client.

Rule 2:7 Conflict of Interest

An investigator should not work for a client if that employment jeopardizes an investigation for another client.

Comment

Loyalty to a client supersedes accepting any work from another client that would adversely affect the original client. An investigator should avoid engaging in cases that will create a conflict of a personal nature, or infringe upon the working relationship already established with a previous client.

Clarification
[1] Working against a previous client

(a) An investigator should not use knowledge gained during the course of any investigation for any client to the detriment or disadvantage of another. Proprietary intelligence gleaned through confidential utterances or from investigative results is the property of only one client.

(b) Information gained during any investigation should not be used by the investigator to the disadvantage of the client. Confidential information disclosed during a previous investigation should not be used for the benefit of another client. This would constitute a breach of confidentiality.

(c) Information about one client must never be shared with another. This has the potential for dire consequences and must be avoided. Information is privileged and should be respected under the rules of confidentiality (see Rule 2:6, Confidentiality).

(d) If such representation innocently occurs, the investigator should withdraw as quickly as possible, to ensure that no information regarding the original client is transmitted to the newer client. It is possible that, after the passage of time, an investigator may contract to perform a service for an individual who is later identified as a party in a previous matter. If this occurs, the investigator should remove him- or herself as soon as the conflict becomes known, ensuring that the confidences of both parties remain intact.

(e) Client contact is confidential. Information gleaned during an investigator/client relationship, no matter how brief, cannot be used against that client by the investigator to further another individual's case. Even limited communication regarding engagement that does not end in work being performed is confidential between the investigator and the inquirer.

(f) There is a limited exception to this rule. It is conceivable that a previous client or case may have gained public notoriety. In such instances general information that does not breach confidentiality may be discussed with or used for the benefit of a new client. Specific information pertinent to a former client or case file may not be revealed. The working relationship between the previous client and the investigator is a matter of confidentiality.

[2] Working for two parties in the same matter

(a) An investigator should not work for opposing parties in the same litigation. An investigator should not knowingly represent two parties in the same or substantially related matter in which their interests are adverse to one another. Such representation would constitute a conflict of interest.

(b) Sharing of information in such an instance would be highly improper because it would necessitate a breach of confidentiality and promote the possibility of bias or prejudice toward one client.

(c) The investigator cannot harm any client by using information known about that client or that client's case for the benefit of another.

[3] Investigations against parties known

(a) An investigator should use clear judgment in the

investigation of a person or persons known to him or her. The consequences of engaging in such action may affect future personal or working relationships.

(b) An investigator must prevent undue prejudice that might result in slanted or untruthful finding of fact. Prior knowledge of an individual may color the veracity of evidence and render findings of fact inaccurate.

(c) It is conceivable that such a situation may unwittingly occur, in which an investigator unknowingly contracts to perform investigation upon an individual known to him or her. In such cases, the investigator should withdraw from the investigation as soon as feasible to avoid jeopardizing either the client's case or the personal relationship.

(d) In a situation of this nature, it is also imperative the investigator not reveal to the subject the fact that an investigation is ongoing, even if he or she has withdrawn from the investigation. Limited contact with the client still establishes a relationship of a confidential nature precluding any revelations to any party in an investigation.

[4] Exception

(a) An exception to the conflict of interest rule may arise when the initial client has revealed the fact and content of the investigation and agrees to the investigator's employment by another party. If the information gleaned by an investigator has been made public in a court of law, through depositions or the resolution of the matter, it is possible that the initial client may not object to information from his or her file being revealed for the benefit of a previous adversary.

(b) Such conflicts should be discussed with each party involved. Once the initial client has approved the disclosure, it is possible to discuss the situation with each party and to agree on the terms under which information from one client may be used to the benefit of another.

(c) Consent should be obtained from each party involved before embarking on any new investigative work. Each party must fully understand the consequences of his or her approval and the possible dangers of allowing work to commence.

(d) It is always suggested that such consent be in writing to avoid future controversy.

Rule 2:8 Truthfulness and Accuracy

It is incumbent upon the investigator to be truthful and accurate in advertising, in dealings with clients, in reporting findings, and in communications to any tribunal, court or law enforcement agency.

<u>Comment</u>

There are many levels of truthfulness and many circumstances in which it should be exercised by the investigator. The investigator should be truthful in business practices. Truth in advertising, honest dealings with clients and accurate representation of information affect the investigator-client relationship. This further extends to truthfulness in reporting the results of all work performed. The consequences of an investigator's findings affect the client for whom services are being performed. The investigator has a duty to inform the client of all findings truthfully and accurately. The job of the investigator is not to create evidence or information, but to find and obtain whatever evidence and information does exist.

Clarification

[1] Truthfulness to the client

(a) The investigator must truthfully represent himself or herself to the client, providing accurate information about experience, education and abilities. Accurate information must be provided to allow the client to make informed decisions about which individual to hire and the extent of services to be provided (see Rule 1:2, Certification and Rule 1:6, Advertising).

(b) The investigator should endeavor to explain all facets of the work to be performed. In addition, the client should understand the possibility of obtaining information and evidence before the investigator undertakes the assignment. Clients are often victims of misinformation. They frequently maintain false perceptions of an investigator's abilities. The extent to which an investigator is able to assist a client should be accurately represented. The client should not be misled to believe that results would occur if this were not a fact (see Rule 2:1, Scope of Employment).

(c) The investigator should frankly inform the client of the consequences of performing illegal or immoral acts. The investigator is charged with educating the client regarding any known criminal act and its consequences. The investigator's moral reservations regarding an assignment should be revealed to the client. This allows the client to make an informed decision if he or she wishes to pursue a working relationship with the investigator (see Rule 2:1 Scope of Employment).

(d) Frequently the information obtained or the evidence gathered is divergent from that which the client would prefer. The investigator should truthfully and accurately report the results of investigative work to the client even in circumstances when the results are not those expected or desired by the client (see Rule 2:4, Communication).

(e) The client should not knowingly make any statements of a false nature that would mislead the client or cause him or her to believe that a situation is other than it is in reality.

[2] Truthfulness toward the tribunal (court)

(a) An investigator shall not knowingly make any false statement to a tribunal or court of law.

(b) If called upon to testify, an investigator should only respond to questions in a factual manner or discuss information of relevance to the investigative assignment with honesty. Testimony should be accurate and truthful. The investigator is an employed worker who has performed a service. The results of this service are necessary for a fact finder, tribunal or court to render informed decisions. The investigator is not an advocate for the cause of the client and should not exaggerate, emphasize or in any way slant his or her findings.

(c) The investigator must be candid and honest without lying or misleading. To the extent that confidentiality can be maintained regarding a client and investigative work for the client, it should be maintained.

(d) False statements are not condoned. An investigator should not knowingly mislead or falsely represent the information or evidence produced during an investigation. Accuracy implies honesty. Neither exaggeration nor minimization is truthful reporting of fact.

[3] Entrapment[9] is not to be exercised or condoned

(a) It is not the responsibility of an investigator to entice or suggest to an individual to engage in conduct not normally within his or her realm of action. It is not the investigator's job to create a situation that would not otherwise exist in furtherance of an investigation.

(b) An investigator should not engage in entrapment or induce any person to perform in a manner contrary to his or her normal behavior for the purpose of advancing the investigator's own case. Placing the idea of action into the mind of an individual who would not otherwise have such thoughts or ideas should not be done to instigate or promote observable activity by the investigator.

[4] Truthfulness in reporting

(a) All information reported to the client should be truthful and accurate. Information should not be falsified or exaggerated. The client deserves all knowledge gleaned by the investigator in spite of its anticipated or expected results. Intelligence learned by the investigator is of consequence to the client. The client deserves accurate reporting of findings upon which to base informed decisions.

(b) Information obtained by the investigator should be truthfully and accurately provided to the client's counsel when requested. This is, of course, contingent upon a client's approval to communicate with his or her attorney (see Rule 2:6, Confidentiality). All information obtained during the course of the investigation is to be transmitted regardless of its positive or negative nature. The client's counsel is properly armed to provide representation when she or he is fully informed. It is not the duty of the investigator to create or bias information. Attorneys representing clients deserve to be fully informed so as to prevent surprises in court.

[5] Fairness to all parties

(a) An investigator should not falsify evidence or counsel a client to do so. Information, evidence and intelligence should be actually that which is extant. No information should be fabricated.

(b) Investigators may not induce, entice or bribe any person for the purpose of obtaining a statement or testimony that is not accurate and true. Payment for information from witnesses is not acceptable behavior. Reluctant witnesses should be reported as such to the client or attorney, but not induced to provide testimony by promise of remuneration or favor.

Rule 2:9 To Do No Harm

The investigator should be constantly mindful of the welfare of others, taking care to not knowingly do harm to any person.

Comment

It is understood that the findings of an investigation may not be beneficial to the party or parties under investigation. The concept of harm extends to any action by the investigator that would inflict physical injury or injury to reputation or well-being as a result of a conscious and purposeful act. Harmful acts include wrongfully disseminating information to inappropriate parties, perpetuating untruths or causing any person to be physically injured.

<u>Clarification</u>

[1] Physical well-being

    (a) The investigator should refrain from using devices or techniques in such a manner that threatens life, limb or safety of others. This includes driving responsibly in order to avoid injury to bystanders during the course of surveillance. It further extends to appropriate use of equipment to prevent physical injury or threat to life and limb.

    (b) The safety of the public is of the utmost concern at all times. Investigators should use all equipment in a responsible and cautious manner. The rights and privileges of every citizen should be taken into account while conducting an investigation. Motor vehicles, firearms and other equipment that could be physically dangerous should be employed with extreme caution and proper training.

    (c) Industry-specific equipment necessary in gathering evidence should be used without threatening the life, limb or safety of any person. Such related equipment includes, but is not limited to, motor vehicles, surveillance equipment, photographic equipment, computers, chemicals for gathering, testing and analysis, polygraph machinery and other apparatus specifically designed to aid the investigator in his or her pursuit of information.

[2] Harm to reputation

    (a) An investigator should not injure the reputation of his or her client. Breach of confidentiality is potentially dangerous to the client's welfare. Discussing the case of a client in an inappropriate situation may prove harmful as well.

(b) The investigator should be aware of the potential damage that can be done by revealing information of a confidential nature to anyone other than the client. Psychological as well as physical harm may result from a breach of contract. The dissemination of privileged information may affect personal relationships and business alliances.

(c) Disclosure of an investigation places the client in jeopardy. The target or subject of an investigation may act or react to this revelation in a manner that ultimately harms the client.

(d) The reputation of the client should be upheld and respected. The client should never be maligned or spoken of in a demeaning manner. False statements should not be uttered and details of financial relationships should not be revealed. An exception arises when fee information is necessarily revealed in a court of law or during dispute resolution between client and investigator.

[3] Use of force

(a) The investigator should never employ force or violence in the execution of his or her duties.

(b) There is never any reason to employ force of any type in the work conducted by the investigator unless she or he, or anyone else is threatened and in fear of bodily harm or loss of life. An investigator is not prevented from defending himself or herself or others.

(c) The work of the investigator is not that of the law

enforcement officer and should never be confused as such. Investigators who have proper licenses to carry firearms should do so responsibly and use them in accordance with the law.

(d) There are no rights or privileges that allow the investigator to inflict physical injury upon any person. An exception would occur if self defense or defense of another were necessary.

[4] Use of information

(a) The investigator should responsibly use information obtained during the course of his or her work. Information should be confidentially maintained and should not be revealed to any party other than the client.

(b) Such revelation may prove harmful to the client. Information should not be obtained for any purpose contrary to law. The investigator potentially harms the public by such activity and defames the investigative community.

(c) Personal or private data gathered on any individual should be obtained legally. Finding information or investigating individuals should be done by methods that comply with existing laws. No information should be obtained illegally. Unscrupulous brokers of information should be avoided.

(d) Information should comply with the dictates of existing law and its interpretation. These are ever changing. The investigator has a responsibility to know the applicable rules governing his or her vocation.

(e) Personal or private data should not be given to anyone

other than the client. An exception may be made when permission is granted by the client or in compliance with a subpoena to testify at a deposition, trial or before a tribunal of fact finders.

[5] Placing a person in jeopardy

(a) An investigation may not knowingly place anyone in harm. An investigator should be cognizant of the motive of the client, if possible. Clients are not always truthful. The possibility exists that an investigator's research is ultimately intended by the client for the purpose of identifying, locating and inflicting injury or death upon another. Motives of clients may not be honestly stated.

(b) To protect all persons from harm, it becomes incumbent upon the investigator to accurately identify the client. In the event of future action, it is the duty of the investigator to make a due diligent effort to maintain information about the client that could be used to identify and/or locate the client at a later time.[10]

(c) It is impossible for the investigator to understand the true motives of any client, however, a reasonable effort should be made to determine the client's need to locate or survey any person. This may include, but is not limited to, inquiries and may involve a signed contract stating the client's intentions with regard to the information.

(d) Locating persons for the execution of judgments or service of process may require the investigator to find an address of residence or workplace. This information is not for public consumption but becomes a part of the confidential file maintained for an individual client.

(e) There is no known legislation regarding procedure for locating an individual.[11]

Rule 2:10 Courtesy to the Client and to the Public

Courtesy and civility are to be extended to all clients and to the public.

Comment

Client relations are often the most difficult part of an investigative assignment. The investigator's inability to handle the client's personality does not forgive discourtesy or incivility. The investigator must act and interact with the public on a daily basis during the course of his or her work. Interviews are conducted, information is obtained, and individuals are communicated with for purposes of finding or reporting information. The investigator should always be mindful of the image he or she portrays when dealing with the public. Courtesy and civility are always expected.

Clarification

[1] Client's state of mind

(a) All clients have problems to be addressed by an investigator. It is the basis for the investigator-client relationship. The client's need for investigative services is based upon an unresolved conclusion to an existing dilemma or controversy. The client is often confused, desperate or panicked. The client is therefore seeking assistance outside of his or her own capabilities. The client is often reticent or reluctant. Clients may be demanding or dictatorial. In spite of the client's demeanor toward the investigator, for whatever cause, the investigator is to be civil toward the client.

(b) The investigator should be mindful of the importance a client places upon his or her unique investigative needs. These situations may be routine for the investigator who is constantly involved in such activity, but they are new, often frightening and stressful for the client. The investigator should be considerate of the client and polite during all interactions.

(c) The investigator owes the client civility. Clients frequently have expectations that are unreasonable because they lack knowledge or education on the true nature of an investigator's ability. The very nature of an investigator-client relationship is one of need. The investigator is the individual (or agency) who is being requested to obtain information and evidence that is needed or desired by the client. A dependency is established between and among these parties. The investigator should be ever mindful of the reliance a client places upon his or her services.

(d) If for any reason, the investigator does not wish to work with a particular client, he or she may refer the client to other resources.

(e) It is not always possible for a client and investigator to maintain a working relationship. Personalities may impair the investigator's ability to properly serve a client. The investigator must always be civil even when the client and the investigator are unable to pursue a working relationship.

(f) Civility and courtesy do not imply intimacy or friendship. It is not necessary for the investigator to pursue any relationship beyond a courteous and respectful working relationship.

[2] Demanding or unreasonable clients

(a) Clients frequently demand an investigator's time and energy above and beyond the work that is being performed. It is not uncommon for a client in desperate need of information to become unreasonably possessive of an investigator's time and energy.

(b) The investigator should explain adequately to each client his or her role as service provider, not friend or psychologist. Demands upon the investigator's time are only reasonable when they advance the case under investigation or are needed to communicate with the client about progress.

(c) Reasonable communication should be established (see Rule 2:4, Communication) and maintained so that the client does not impede the progress of an investigation or encroach on the investigator's private time.

(d) The investigator should courteously inform the client of the terms of their relationship. He or she should avoid being rude or acrimonious to a client.

(e) There are no rules governing the manner in which a client must treat an investigator. It is unfortunate that civility cannot be forced on all parties. However, in spite of a client's lack of civility, the investigator is charged with the responsibility of maintaining a dignified demeanor.

[3] Courtesy and civility toward the public

(a) The investigator should be mindful of the impression he or she makes in public. Acting in a manner that is thoughtful and considerate is appropriate demeanor.

(b) Casual inquiries by the public about the investigator's work should be handled with deference and respect. Requests for the investigator to explain his or her profession should be heeded and appropriate responses provided.

(c) Investigators frequently interact with the public in the furtherance of an investigation. Interviews are conducted of individuals with knowledge of or relevance to a situation under investigation. These persons are to be treated with respect. Communication should be polite and civil, never demanding or threatening. Sometimes a person may prefer not to speak with an investigator or become involved in an ongoing investigation. In spite of this reluctance, the investigator should always be polite and respectful to any person.

(d) The investigator must interact with many persons during the course of records retrieval and document research. Often these individuals are overworked and underpaid members of bureaucratic agencies. Obtaining cooperation from such persons is often difficult. The investigator should always be mindful of his or her duty to represent the profession respectfully and responsibly, in spite of the demeanor of the individuals from whom requests are made.

(e) The image of the investigator should be upheld even when it is difficult to maintain a countenance of civility.

(f) An investigator's behavior in a court of law or in the presence of representatives for opposing sides to an issue under investigation should be stellar. The investigator should be respectful and civil to all parties at all times.

(g) This respect should be displayed not only in word, but also in the investigator's dress and deportment, showing respect for the court system.

Rule 2:11 Personal Bias

Personal prejudice, bias, and political or religious beliefs should not be permitted to interfere with the faithful and honest discharge of an investigator's duty.

Comment

At all times the investigator should endeavor to be fair and open minded with respect to all parties involved in an investigation. Personal preferences and affiliations should not influence the search or the reporting of fact.

Clarification

[1] Investigator-client bias

(a) Investigator-client bias is to be avoided. It is possible that an investigator may not prefer the client's personality, moral, religious or political beliefs. He or she is still entrusted with performing work diligently. Like or dislike of a client should not affect excellence in work.

(b) The investigator works for, but does not necessarily assume the same preferences or proclivities of, his or her client. The investigator is an unbiased finder of fact and may be retained by a person or persons with whom there is no shared belief, ethic or morality.

(c) Employment of an investigator by a client is not an

endorsement of the client's proclivities or beliefs. Neither does it imply a shared philosophy or lifestyle.

(d) If an investigator is so personally biased against a particular client for reasons such as (but not limited to) ethnic or racial origin, political or religious preference, belief or ideology that he or she cannot properly perform a service for the client, then the investigator should withdraw from the working relationship. The quality of the work should not be jeopardized. All clients deserve an adequate opportunity to satisfy their investigative requests without interference or limitation due to the personal preferences of an investigator.

(e) Work for the client should never be inadequate or of lesser quality because of the investigator's personal feelings toward the client. Once an investigator contracts to perform work it becomes his or her duty to carry out each assignment with diligence, honesty and integrity.

[2] Bias in conducting an investigation

(a) There should never be bias in conducting an investigation. All cases should be investigated with a fair and open-minded attitude that will allow the search for truth to surmount any other consideration. Extreme like or dislike for the subject under investigation must not interfere with a neutral, open-minded evaluation of all information and data.

(b) The client's cause is not necessarily the investigator's cause. The investigator is a finder of fact related to an issue of importance to the client. He or she is not necessarily motivated by the same set of criteria as the client. Although the investigator is not necessarily espousing the same

> ideology as the client, it is still his or her job to seek information by reasonable investigative means.

(c) The investigator should not allow predisposition, prejudice or bias to interfere with the pursuit of truth. All avenues should be pursued even when odious or offensive to an investigator.

(d) The investigator is a non-prejudiced reporter of fact. Evidence gained should not be slanted, tainted or skewed by predisposition of the investigator. Personal like or dislike has no place in the reporting of findings.

(e) Personal dislike or opposing philosophies should never color the results of an investigation.

Rule 2:12 Records Maintenance

The client's property should be preserved separately and safely, apart from other property in the investigator's possession. All client files and records should be securely segregated and beyond access by noninvolved parties. Appropriate precautions in the form of firewalls, passwords or other current state of the art controls should be used for all computer stored records. Investigators should maintain a system of record keeping that allows information to be retrieved for a reasonable time after the work has been completed.

Comment

Information and evidence that is the property of a client should be held with a fiduciary responsibility. Records should be maintained for a reasonable time so as to be available for the client's need. It is reasonable to retain records such as case files, evidence and related documentation for at least three years, but seven years would be optimal. There is no mandate or dictate assigned to this period of record retention.

Clarification

[1] File maintenance

(a) The investigator is charged with retaining case files, working notes, evidence and related documentation for use by the client or attorney. This material may be maintained in a variety of media including, but not limited to, paper files, computer files on hard drive, or other storage device, film, or video. As technology advances the current and appropriate file storage system should be maintained in a secure manner. Original evidence should be maintained in its original state whenever possible. Photocopied documentation of evidence is less valuable than the original evidence.

(b) These records are proof of work performed and the results of such service. They should be maintained in the normal system that constitutes the regular business practices of the investigator. Working notes, case information, evidence, results and reports should be held in a safe and secure manner to assure that they may be retrieved and used when necessary by the client.

(c) These materials are all confidential, case-related private documents (see Rule 2:6, Confidentiality) and are not the same as records requested or required by Internal Revenue Service or other tax-related entities for proof of income. They should be maintained separately from an investigator's personal files and records and secured from any non-involved party.

(d) Proof of income, expenses and related documents should be separately maintained in accordance with federal, state or local rules and regulations. Payroll records and federal, state and local tax records should be stored apart from records related to the private and confidential documents that are the subject of an investigative case file.

(e) Before destroying any documents related to a particular file it is incumbent upon the investigator to ensure that such file materials are no longer required for proof of facts by a client or attorney for purposes of litigation.

(f) Files in matters of post-conviction or cases of on-going litigation matters should not be destroyed as long as the case is open or pending further action. It would behoove the investigator to maintain contact with the attorney of record to guarantee the availability of necessary documents and investigation.

[2] Notification of destruction

(a) No evidence should be destroyed without first communicating with legal counsel to determine if it will be relevant at a later date.

(b) No original documentation or evidence should be destroyed without the same communication or confirmation.

(c) In lieu of specific communication about the destruction of files, the investigator may disclose his or her file retention practices to each client. This allows the client to anticipate the length of time that information and material will be available and places the burden on the client to request any extensions.

(d) It is unrealistic to expect that an investigator will retain all files indefinitely. Unless otherwise requested by a client, it is appropriate to properly dispense of file information at a reasonable time after the work is concluded.

[3] Method of destruction

(a) Destruction of records should be done in a manner that does not jeopardize the confidentiality of a client.

(b) Files and records should be destroyed by shredding, burning or other means sufficient to render them indecipherable.

(c) Disposal of private information from a client's case file should never jeopardize confidentiality. This is true even when the working relationship was terminated many years before.

(d) Ongoing criminal files or lengthy litigation files with potential for multiple appeals should not be destroyed without approval of the client and/or legal counsel.

[4] Exceptions

(a) Exceptions to the rule apply when a case is not considered for litigation and the evidence is reproducible.

(b) Destruction of documents that are a part of the public record is appropriate. These are materials (such as deeds, mortgages, birth and death records, etc.) that can be reproduced or obtained again at another time.

(c) Regulations within the legal community vary from state to state. The primary guideline is to not prejudice a client's future case(s) or judicial decisions because of deprivation of file material. Each investigator is advised to determine the rule for his/her individual jurisdiction and follow that determinate number of years.

(c) If an investigation has been concluded and a minimum of three years has elapsed without the client's requesting additional work, it is appropriate to destroy file materials without asking the client for approval as long as the client has been informed at the commencement of the work that this is the policy of the investigator.

Rule 2:13 Terminating a Working Relationship

An investigator's service for a client shall cease when either party has withdrawn from the working relationship and clearly informed the other that all work will be terminated. The relationship may be terminated by either the investigator or the client.

<u>Comment</u>

An investigator may elect to terminate a relationship for criminal or ethical reasons or because he or she has experienced a financial hardship due to the client's inability or refusal to pay for services. Clients may elect to withdraw from a working relationship with an investigator for a multitude of reasons. These are outside of the authority or responsibility of this code. In either circumstance, the investigator must still maintain the confidences of the client except when criminal activity has been discovered or to protect the life, limb or safety of an individual.

<u>Clarification</u>
[1] Investigator's rationale for withdrawal
(a) If an investigator believes or discovers that a client's

conduct is adverse to the law or the rules of conduct, he or she may terminate the relationship. The investigator has no obligation to a client or any other person to participate in criminal activity.

(b) If an investigator discovers that he or she has been employed to further a client's criminal activity, withdrawal is essential. The client's true intent or purpose may not be revealed until an investigation is underway. When nefarious intent is discovered, the investigator should withdraw.

(c) A client has a duty to pay an investigator for work performed. If and when a client has shown sufficient reluctance or inability to fulfill his or her portion of the working relationship, the investigator may terminate the relationship. An investigator should not suffer financial hardship to further the benefit of a client.

(d) If a client desires to pursue a course of action that is adverse to the investigator, the relationship may be concluded. The investigator is under no obligation to perform work that is odious or offensive.

(e) An investigator may terminate a working relationship if she or he feels incapable of serving the client's best interests. Inexperience, time constraints or ethical beliefs may hinder a working relationship with a client.

(f) An investigator may withdraw from a matter under investigation if she or he believes that the client's actions endanger an investigation or jeopardize the investigator's health, welfare or safety.

[2] Client's request for termination of services

(a) A client may, at any time, terminate the services of an investigator. No reason or rationale is necessary for such action. The client has no duty to explain this action to the investigator.

(b) A client has the prerogative to terminate the services of an investigator at any time. An investigator has no power over the actions of a client.

(c) Clients are responsible for fees incurred up to the time of termination. Collection of debt should be conducted in a manner that is legally acceptable and generally approved within the code of professional conduct.

[3] Investigators action upon separation

(a) An investigator who has been discharged from an assignment by the client should terminate all work for that client. The information and evidence amassed during the course of the investigation are still subject to the rules of confidentiality (see Rule 2:6, Confidentiality).

(b) No additional billing should be accumulated after the conclusion of a working relationship, except where allowed (see Rule 2:5, Fees).

Investigator-Investigator Relations

Rule 3:1 Responsibilities of an Investigator, Agency Owner, or License Qualifier

The investigator must make reasonable efforts to ensure that all persons working with or for him or her adhere to the same rules and abide by the law in the same manner as the investigator.

<u>Comment</u>

It is the responsibility of the agency owner, licensed investigator or supervisory person in an investigative agency to assure that any persons working with or for him or her abide by rules of confidentiality, honesty and diligence. The investigator should impress upon his or her employees and co-workers the need to adhere to the same code of professional conduct by which he or she abides. Client confidentiality is no less important for the administrative or secretarial staff of an investigator's office than for the investigator.

<u>Clarification</u>

[1] Owner's or supervisor's responsibility

(a) A supervising investigator should make every reasonable effort to impress upon those persons working with or under his or her direction that the same laws and rules of conduct bind them all. Each member of an agency or partner in an assignment should adhere to the same ethics and rules of conduct.

(b) An investigator or agency owner shall be responsible for the actions of his or her employees, subcontracted workers or partners. When that owner or investigator has knowledge of conduct that is in violation of the rules of professional conduct it is incumbent upon him or her to ensure such actions cease.

(c) An owner or supervisor must not order any subordinate, subcontractor, partner or employee to violate the code of professional conduct. It is his or her duty to instruct subordinates only to perform tasks that are lawful.

(d) The owner or supervising investigator is responsible if she or he knowingly condones activity by an employee or subcontractor that violates the code of conduct or any law. Knowledge that an employee or coworker is violating the law requires that the supervising investigator immediately take corrective action.

(e) A supervising investigator with knowledge of an employee's or coworker's violation of the law or a code of conduct has a responsibility to ameliorate the situation to the best of his or her ability. Such action should not be allowed to continue. Any misrepresentation or action that is reparable should be corrected.

(f) The highest level of service can only be attained if all members of an agency or partners in an investigation are instructed as to the standards of conduct expected of them. Confidentiality of information, legal methods of investigation and adherence to rules and regulations affecting investigators should be understood by everyone involved in an agency's work.

[2] Request for work that is inappropriate

(a) No investigator should request another to do work that is either unlawful, immoral or potentially dangerous to life or physical well-being.

(b) An investigator in need of assistance by an employee or subcontracted employee should not knowingly subject that individual to an assignment that is unlawful. No person working with or for an investigator should be instructed to violate any law. The investigator is charged with the responsibility of maintaining current information on laws affecting the profession.

(c) An investigator should be aware of the moral constraints of all work to be performed and should not request that any individual perform immoral work. Morality is subjective and open to individual interpretation. However, any demand for work by another who has expressed a belief adverse to the moral necessities of the assignment should not be forced to engage in such action.

(d) An investigator should not knowingly place another investigator in harm's way. Every effort should be made to protect the health and welfare of all investigators assisting in an assignment.

(e) Proper registration with state licensing authorities is mandatory. State laws vary with regard to registration of an investigative agency's ancillary workers. It is the responsibility of the investigator or agency owner to properly adhere to local licensing laws and restrictions (see Rule 1:1, Licensing).

Rule 3:2 Partner, Employee or Subcontractor Responsibilities

All individuals working with or for an investigator are expected to adhere to the same rules of conduct demanded of the investigator.

<u>Comment</u>

Many investigative agencies are comprised of two or more individuals working in concert, under employment agreements or as subcontractors to agency owners. These persons are charged with the same responsibilities of adhering to the law and abiding by the code of conduct as the investigator or agency owner with whom they work. This extends to non-investigative staff as well.

<u>Clarification</u>

[1] Adherence to rules

    (a) Every reasonable effort should be made by the supervising investigator or agency owner to impress upon all employees the need to adhere to the same code of conduct and abide by all existing laws (see Rule 3:1, Responsibilities of an investigator, agency owner, or license qualifier).

    (b) All persons working with or for another investigator or agency should aspire to adhere to the same code of ethics as the investigator or agency for whom she or he works. It is the duty of all persons to abide by the law of the land. It is the responsibility of individuals within the specialized world of the investigator to protect the client and work product of the investigative agency.

    (c) All persons working with or for another investigator are bound by the same restrictions regarding confidentiality, conflict of interest, honesty and expediency as the licensed investigator or agency for whom he or she works. The ultimate responsibility falls upon the licensee (or active investigator), but does not eliminate the need for adjunct staff to live up to the standards imposed upon their primary employer.

(d) Confidentiality agreements are suggested as a manner by which employees and co-workers can be made aware of the importance and seriousness of their position. A document outlining the terms of a working relationship serves the dual purpose of informing the employee or co-worker and affirming that client confidentiality will be maintained.

[2] Employee and subcontractor responsibility

(a) It is the duty of all investigators to understand the laws that affect licensing. It is the responsibility of all investigators to perform work according to the highest ethical standards. No employee, subcontractor or partner is relieved of responsibility for violation of accepted rules of conduct.

(b) An employee, subcontractor or partner cannot be ordered to do something that is illegal or unethical. That individual has the responsibility to decline such assignment.

[3] Adherence to the rules of professional conduct should extend to all non-investigative employees as well as those who are licensed.

(a) Those working with or for an investigator or investigative agency do so with the understanding that the work they are performing ultimately affects the lives of the clients whom it serves. There is an implied awareness of the exceptional nature of the work performed that requires loyalty to the employer and protection of the client. The nature of the work itself suggests a responsibility toward exceptional care.

(b) Every individual working in any capacity for an investigator or agency should be mindful of the need for confidentiality, truthfulness and accuracy in reporting. This should be stressed by the employer (licensee or agency owner) and adhered to by the employee or adjunct staff member.

(c) Conflicts of interest extend to persons working for an investigator or investigative agency and should be immediately reported to prevent any appearance of impropriety. That person or persons should withdraw from work on a particular assignment and avoid involvement with any portion of that work. In extreme cases it might be advisable for the agency to decline an assignment that might prove to have adverse consequences because of an employee with a conflict of interest.

(d) Persons within an agency who experience a conflict of interest are precluded from discussing the matter with any person outside of the agency. Confidentiality extends to the names of clients and the specific nature of work being performed by the agency.

(e) Confidentiality agreements are suggested as a prudent method of ensuring the discretion of non-investigative employees.

Rule 3:3 Subcontractor Regulations

A subcontractor is forbidden to contact the primary client directly unless authorized by the contracting firm.

Comment

The subcontractor is an independent investigator working for another investigator for limited assignments. That person has responsibilities to his or her investigator employer to work with the same diligence and concern as if the client were his or her own. An investigator hired to execute a duty as an independent contractor has all of the responsibilities of performing that work to the highest level of ability with all due diligence and timeliness. The results of his or her work product, however, become the property of the employing investigator. Communication with the client or solicitation of the client is forbidden except under specific circumstances.

Clarification

[1] Client contact

(a) An investigator hired as a subcontractor is forbidden to make contact with the primary client for any purpose (reporting, asking questions, confirming information or other reason) without first obtaining authorization and approval from the contracting investigator or investigative agency.

(b) It is suggested that such authority be in writing.[12] The purpose of this document is to protect all parties in the event of a future dispute.

(c) The subcontracting investigator should not interfere with the working relationship established between the client and investigator who has been retained for services. Any communication, attempt to solicit the client, or discussion about the primary investigator's ability is forbidden.

Rule 3:4 Reputation of Other Investigators

An investigator will not directly or indirectly inhibit the future prospects or adversely affect the practice of another investigator.

Comment

An investigator will not injure the professional reputation of another investigator by speaking untruths, making malicious statements or spreading rumors.

Clarification

An investigator will not engage in any activity, word or deed that injures the professional reputation of another investigator.

[1] Malicious words

(a) Rumors about the quality of work, work habits and practices of another investigator should not be spread or encouraged. Unless an activity is known to be criminal or unethical, investigators are encouraged to limit negative or critical communication about others in the profession except to report unethical behavior to the appropriate forum (see Rule 3:4, Clarification [2]b, Reporting unethical behavior).

(b) Investigators are individuals with individualized methods of work. The work of the investigator is not limited by specific dictates as to method and manner of approach. All consideration for the individualized work of an investigative colleague should be made when discussing that person in a professional context.

(c) An investigator should not criticize the work of another except for the purposes of discussion or critique in the appropriate forum.

[2] Reporting unethical behavior

(a) Unethical behavior of another investigator should be reported to the appropriate forum to ensure that all investigators perform the highest quality of work.

(b) The appropriate forum for reporting the unethical or unprofessional actions of another investigator may consist of a police entity, a court system, state licensing authority or professional association ethics board.

Rule 3:5 Payment of Work by Other Investigators

Investigators should compensate each other appropriately and expediently for work performed.

<u>Comment</u>

An investigator should ever be mindful of the need to compensate fellow investigators in a timely manner for work performed on his or her behalf. The erratic manner in which clients are obtained and cases are completed is the nature of the profession. Investigators are subject to a variety of economic, social and political situations that affect the regular flow of work and caseloads. Most investigators working independently experience this frustration. It is therefore incumbent upon the investigator to be sensitive to the needs of a colleague who has extended himself or herself to perform a work assignment.

Clarification
[1] Remuneration

(a) Investigators should be timely and responsible in their compensation of other investigators for work performed.

(b) Agreements, either oral or in writing, should be made before one investigator begins work for another. The method, manner and timeliness of remuneration should be understood and agreed upon by both parties. An investigator should expect payment immediately upon completion of an assignment unless otherwise agreed upon. In some situations, the investigator may be employed with the understanding that payment will be delayed until the primary investigator has been paid by the client. Work should not be performed without a full understanding of the specific arrangements for payment for services rendered.

(c) Investigators should set an example for all clients by promptly remunerating each other for work performed.

(d) No investigator should be expected to work without compensation unless he or she has agreed to pro bono employment before performing the assignment. A subcontracting investigator should be paid by the primary investigator even if the primary is not compensated by the client.

[2] Industry discounts and professional courtesy

(a) Industry discounts are encouraged, but not demanded. Investigators network to optimize the quality of work product and results for clients. Professional discounts on services and fees are suggested.

(b) Gratitude for such courtesy should be properly rewarded by timely payment at the conclusion of the assignment.

(c) Payment is not contingent upon such courtesy. It is expected as a necessity to fulfill a contract for work performed.

Rule 3:6 Multiple Investigators Working in Concert

Responsibilities and reimbursement of each investigator should be clarified and confirmed before beginning an assignment. Responsibility and credit should be shared with all parties.

Comment

Clarification of the duties and responsibilities of all individuals involved in multi- investigator assignments should be confirmed before work is begun. The involvement of two or more investigators working together on the same assignment necessitates a clear understanding between the participants. All work anticipated and the method of reimbursement should be fully specified. Credit for work performed should be willingly shared.

Clarification

[1] Written contracts

(a) Written agreements between multiple investigators or agencies are not necessary in multi-investigator assignments. They are, however, suggested as a means of avoiding controversy, defining responsibilities and ensuring the most cooperative work circumstances.

(b) All participants should understand the assignment of tasks before work is begun. The manner of distributing assignments should be mutually agreed upon with the client's best interests as the ultimate goal.

(c) Duplication of effort should be avoided to ensure the client is not overcharged. Investigators involved in such cases should be mindful to avoid replication of work that does not benefit the client. Fair and considerate effort should be made so that the client is not penalized because of inadequate preparation on the part of the investigators.

[2] Exceptions

(a) If the assignment is being controlled by an attorney or client who delegates assignments, then the investigators have no control over the possibility of duplication of time and effort.

(b) Each investigator should make his or her abilities known to the controlling administrator to assist in the decision-making process. Investigators may suggest or advise based upon their experience and knowledge. Ultimate authority in such cases is the responsibility of the attorney or client.

[3] Credit for work performed

(a) Affirmative results should be credited appropriately to all individuals working on the matter. No one investigator should be credited with the success of an investigation when the effort was shared by others.

(b) An exception to this occurs when an investigator chooses to remain anonymous for reasons of personal safety or to continue work on this or other matters without his or her identity being revealed.

Rule 3:7 Competition between Investigators

An investigator should not interfere with business contracts between other investigators and their clients.

Comment

Solicitation of work and advertising by the investigator should be done legally and fairly.

Clarification

[1] Unscrupulous solicitation

(a) An investigator should not use inappropriate or unscrupulous methods to take clients away from another investigator.

(b) Any illegal action is beyond the scope of proper activity of an investigator, including but not limited to the solicitation of work.

(c) The concept of fairness should be used in the solicitation of work by and between any investigator.

[2] Contact by clients of another investigator

(a) There is no limit on the number of investigators who may be contacted by any client or potential client for any reason. A client may contact an investigator other than the one whom he or she has previously retained. That other investigator is not culpable of solicitation or in breach of any ethical code.

(b) Any person has the right to solicit the services of an investigator. Regulation of this falls outside of the responsibility of this code.

(c) A client may engage in price and service comparison without placing the onus of unscrupulous solicitation upon the investigator whom she or he has contacted. In such instances the investigator bears no responsibility for inappropriate solicitation of a client.

Rule 3:8 Assistance and Guidance between and for Investigators

Assistance and guidance should be offered to investigators with lesser experience or those in need of help to complete an assignment.

Comment

Investigators are encouraged to offer assistance and guidance to colleagues new to the profession or to those who might benefit from greater experience, education or training.

Clarification

[1] Mentoring and sharing information

(a) Mentoring of newer investigators is encouraged as a means of upgrading the quality of the entire profession. The education of all investigators is not equal. Individuals with experience in the field may direct and guide newer persons to ensure the greatest quality of work for clients.

(b) Sharing information, ideas, sources, and methods promotes the improvement of all areas of the investigative industry. Providing opportunity, education and skill for the professional development and advancement of investigators advances the abilities and public image of all investigators.

(c) Participation in educational programs, seminars and training sessions helps to maintain standards and improve the work skills of investigators. Working within the profession to further educate and train practicing investigators is a service with positive and beneficial consequences for the public and for the profession.

(d) Knowledge is a key to raising the standards for all investigators. It improves work, personal skills and the ability to better serve the public. The lawful exchange of information to increase knowledge provides a basis for improving the results of all future work performed by investigators. This assists the public in the pursuit of information and ensures that investigators do not violate the law during their work.

[2] Affiliation with dishonest investigators

(a) Alliances with investigators whose goals are inconsistent with honest and unbiased investigation is discouraged.

(b) An investigator should avoid working with those who use methods or maintain standards that do not promote the betterment of the profession. In any industry there are persons who abide by existing laws and moral precepts. There are unfortunately those who do not abide by the same code of ethics. These persons demean not only themselves, but also the investigative profession as a whole. Use of the services of persons who provide information in a manner that is criminal or by means that are unethical should be eschewed.

(c) Individuals who knowingly cross the line of that which is legal and acceptable to attain their investigative goals are a discredit to the industry. Investigators should refrain from affiliation with such persons.

Transactions with Other Persons

Rule 4:1 Respect for Rights of Third Persons

The legal rights of all persons are to be respected by the investigator in the pursuit of evidence and information for a client.

Comment

The primary responsibility of an investigator is the pursuit of evidence and information for the benefit of a client. The rights and privileges afforded all other persons should not be violated to attain this end. No person should be placed in danger by the actions of the investigator or treated uncivilly.

Clarification

[1] Violation of the rights of third persons

(a) The investigator should respect the rights of all persons in the course of conducting his or her business. No laws should be broken that will infringe upon the rights of any person.

(b) These rights are too numerous to delineate. The investigator, however, should not jeopardize any constitutional or legal rights of any party to accomplish the goals of an investigation.

Rule 4:2 Communication with Person Represented by Counsel

An investigator working for an attorney or a client who is represented by counsel is precluded from contacting an individual represented by opposing counsel. An investigator should not violate any rules regarding ex parte contact during an investigation.

Comment

The American Bar Association's *Model Rules of Professional Conduct* specifically prohibit an attorney from contacting the client of another lawyer in a matter in which he or she is involved. An investigator working for an attorney becomes an agent of that counselor. By extension, the investigator is also restrained from contacting the client of another lawyer in an adverse action with the investigator's own attorney or client. The rising popularity of social media and internet usage has opened up an entire body of law regarding the appropriateness of access to both represented and non-represented parties. The ability to view both public and private information posted by an individual in a multitude of locations on the internet has brought with it decisions in law and in ethics that must be respected by the investigator.

Clarification

[1] Limitations of contact

(a) This rule refers to communications specific to the matter under investigation. It does not limit communications outside the scope of that representation. Any matter that is separate from the controversy in question cannot be limited.

(b) The investigator is therefore referred to Rule 4.2 of the *American Bar Association Rules of Professional Conduct*[13] for clarification on such issues. It is suggested that any interpretation of these rules be done by the attorney for whom the investigator is working. Responsibility should ultimately fall upon the lawyer to interpret the law and direct the investigator in these matters.

(c) In many states limited contact during *sub rosa* investigations is permitted. The investigator is advised to be aware of existing laws that affect the practice of the profession in a given jurisdiction.

(d) Individual jurisdictions and ethics boards have weighed in on the appropriateness of an investigators access to public postings by an individual on his or her social media platform.[14] The investigator works as an agent of the attorney-client and must abide by the rules of ex parte contact.[15]

Rule 4:3 Communication with Witnesses and Persons being Interviewed

All persons with whom an investigator must communicate regarding a matter under investigation are to be afforded all rights and privileges of any citizen. An investigator should respect and not infringe upon the rights of any person.

Comment

An investigator must interact with a variety of people on a regular basis. No person should be placed in jeopardy or suffer deprivation of any right or privilege at the hand of an investigator.

Clarification

[1] Interviews and statements

(a) No investigator should place any witness or person being interviewed in harm or in fear of life, limb or safety. Every precaution should be taken not to intimidate or threaten any person. Reluctant witnesses may not cooperate to the extent desired by an investigator. However, no person can or should be forced to make statements against his or her will.

(b) The investigator must never provide payment or make promises of future remuneration to any person as an enticement to provide a witness statement. No person should be bribed, induced by reward of any kind or enticed to make any statement that is either true or false. All statements (either verbal or written) should be given freely without promise of reward.

Rule 4:4 Communication Regarding Investigative Services

An investigator should truthfully and accurately represent his or her services to the public. Investigative services and the investigator's abilities should be honestly portrayed.

Comment

Advertising and marketing by the investigator should be performed with honesty. The investigator should not exaggerate his or her skills or tell untruths about work performed to entice or induce any person. Communications should be accurate and correct to provide the public with an opportunity to make informed decisions regarding the possibility of working with an investigator.

Clarification

[1] Marketing and advertising

(a) The investigator should be truthful when marketing his or her services to the public. No misrepresentations should be made regarding ability, experience or skill. The public has the right to accurate information upon which to make informed decisions (see Rule 1:6, Advertising).

(b) The public should not be placed in a position of expecting results based on the inaccurate or untrue advertising of an investigator.

[2] Explanation of services

(a) An investigator should fully explain his or her services to educate the public about the nature and abilities of the profession. Misconceptions and stereotypes abound that do a disservice to the practicing professional investigator. The investigator should help to dispel the myths by not falsifying or exaggerating his or her abilities (see Rule 2:1, Scope of Employment).

(b) An investigator should not advertise credentials that are not earned or current. No certification may be displayed that has not been duly earned and awarded by an appropriate authoritative agency (see Rule 1:2, Certification).

(c) It is inappropriate for an investigator to take credit for work that he or she has not performed. Falsification of information is misleading and unfair to the public. Claiming unearned ability or exaggerating experience discredits the profession and places the client in harm's way (see Rule 1:6, Advertising).

Endnotes

1. Each individual state has its own licensing authority. In some states, the state police govern the activities of investigators and issue licenses. In others, the office of the district attorney has that job. Still others have licensing boards established under a variety of government oversight agencies. Most states provide statewide licensing. See the Appendix for a list of state licensing authorities. Individuals wishing to become investigators in a particular jurisdiction are urged to research the applicable requirements and proper entity to which they must apply for licensing.

2. Professional organizations such as the National Association of Legal Investigators (NALI) offer certification of proficiency in the industry. NALI's Certified Legal Investigator (CLI) standard is currently one of the most prestigious credentials available. Others, such as Certified Fraud Examiner (CFE) and Certified Protection Professional (CPP), also attest to a level of excellence within the profession. A continued interest in enhancing the education of investigators has recently seen additional national and state associations now offering advanced certifications. See the Appendix for a list of available certifications.

3. Changing regulations and ethical decisions impact upon the investigator's ability to use social media sites for gathering information. For example, a 2011 San Diego, CA opinion stated that a lawyer whose client was wrongfully discharged was not able to "friend" other employees of that same company to obtain information. As an agent of the attorney, an investigator has the same prohibitions. A 2009 Philadelphia, PA case involved an attorney hiring an investigator to "friend" a non-party witness on Facebook. The Philadelphia Bar Association Professional Guidance Committee opined that it was an unethical deception for the attorney to surreptitiously gain access by using the investigator to do what he was prohibited from doing. Rule 5.3 of the attorney's Rules of Professional conduct holds the lawyer responsible for conduct of a non-lawyer employee. A 2014 article (Ethical Boundaries on the Lawyer's Use of Social Media, 24 Cornell Journal of Law and Public Policy 145)

discusses a situation where in the New York State Bar Association issued a detailed set of social media guidelines covering a vast range of social media prohibitions based upon "public" versus "non-public" portions of individuals personal accounts online.

4. Alternate words are used to describe one who solicits clients for attorneys. The terms "capper" and "ambulance chaser" are alternative slang for the same occupation as a "runner."

5. Several national associations currently promote the understanding and education of investigators with respect to legislation enacted and proposed on a local, state and federal level. The National Counsel of Investigative and Security Services (NCISS) has become the legislative arm of the investigative profession by concentrating on promoting legislation that is both friendly to the profession and protective of the rights of the citizens for whom investigators work. The increase in educational seminars by state and national associations has combined to offer a greater scope of knowledge to investigators around the world.

6. Ever-advancing methods of evaluating evidence, such as DNA technology, computer information analysis and other specific areas of expertise affect the value of information and evidence gathered by an investigator. If one is to promote oneself as a specialist, he or she must be current and knowledgeable about such information.

7. Hacking is the unauthorized intrusion of another into personal computer files. This can be done remotely without authority and to the detriment of the computer owner. In the case of investigator's files and records, it is of utmost importance that classified and confidential files be maintained safe from intrusion and visibility to those who would seek to use private information for nefarious reasons.

8. The concept of Work Product Privilege is also one of controversy. Changing legislation makes it difficult to properly state what is legal and not at this time. For example, a decision (NY CLS CPLR § 3101) reveals that, "The burden of establishing that the communication sought to be discovered is a 'privileged communication' is upon the party resisting its disclosure and where relationship between a self-

insured cab company and the investigator-adjuster who made a report of the accident for the company and its attorney was not made clear, the defendant must comply with plaintiff's notice for discovery." This is just one current citation of various divergent decisions; thus the investigator is burdened with seeking advice of counsel who will be defending the right to keep records and files confidential.

9. The concept of entrapment is a defense, not an offense, against charges brought by the government or law enforcement agencies. It is used generally as a term to describe the process of "roping" or "setting a trap for" the targeted person.

10. It is also a best practice to obtain identifying information about the client to ensure the ability to again locate this person If the Information they glean from an investigator is used for a nefarious purpose. The investigator should be reasonably certain that they know their client and that they are not aiding or abetting any unlawful act on the part of that person.

11. While there is no law or rule stating the manner in which a person should be located, there is an industry standard that has been widely adopted to protect persons from being harmed. It is good practice to inquire of the client wishing the locate service what his or her purpose is for finding another individual. Then, once that individual is located, it is good practice to inquire if he or she wishes to have their private information shared with the client. This is to protect against real physical injury or intrusion into the privacy of one's life. This may also protect the "found" individual and the investigator from being involved in a potentially dangerous situation wherein physical or mental harm might result. While an adopted child may desire to locate his biological parent, that parent may have viable reasons to avoid contact with the child abandoned decades ago. Standard procedure in cases of locating persons for service of process or execution of judgment does not follow these same standards.

12. A writing may be in the form of a typed or written document, letter, facsimile, e-mail or other record of authority.

13. ABA Model Rules: Rule 4.2 Communication with person represented

by counsel. In representing a client, a lawyer shall not communicate about the subject of the representation with a person the lawyer knows to be represented by another lawyer in the matter, unless the lawyer has the consent of the other lawyer or is authorized by law to do so . . . [3] This Rule also applies to communications with any person, whether or not a party to a formal adjudicative proceeding, contract or negotiation, who is represented by counsel concerning the matter to which the communication relates.

14. Note that there is a difference between observing something posted publicly by an individual on a social media site and information that is private for only invitees to view. The acceptability of "friending" a person on a private site for the purpose of using information against him or her is in dispute and under consideration at this time. It should be remembered that the investigator is always the agent of the attorney-client. If it is not appropriate for the attorney retaining the services of the investigator, then it is not appropriate for the investigator. Due diligence is required.

15. Legal rules regarding ex parte contact refer to communication of an attorney or his/her agent with an individual represented by counsel without having that counsel present. These rules refer to the investigator who is retained as an agent of the attorney-client. Thus, if the attorney cannot ethically or legally approach a represented party, then the investigator is also precluded from doing so.

Terminology

Advertise – To tout, expose and sell a product or personal skill in a public forum.

Agency – A business entity owned by or employing investigators, independent of any law firm, company or corporation.

Attorney – Lawyer. A counselor. One licensed to practice law.

Bias – Predisposition. Slant or prejudice for or against one thing or another. Having made up one's mind prior to completing an investigation. Based on prejudice, not on facts.

Bribes – Inducements or incentives. Usually financial. An investigator must never use bribery to obtain the cooperation of a witness.

Capper – A person who solicits cases for an attorney. Ambulance chasers. (See also: runner.)

Certification – A document attesting to a certain fact. Used in this publication to imply recognition of achievement of a degree, title or higher level of education.

Civil – Referring to ordinary citizens (as opposed to military or ecclesiastical). Especially when referring to conflict, suit resolution or law affecting persons in dispute in a court of equity. As opposed to criminal, which has a court of punitive measures against persons doing harm or wrong.

Compensation – Remuneration. Payment for a service rendered.

Competence – Experience or expertise in a given subject. Establishing qualifications to be capable of a particular ability.

Confidentiality – Intended to be kept secret. To be maintained in trust. Referring to the working relation of an investigator with his or her client. Information relevant to the client is to be kept secret and not to be revealed to any other party.

Conflict of interest – Owing a duty to more than one party, thus preventing proper fulfillment of that duty to either party. An investigator cannot work for opposing parties in litigation.

Contingency fees – Dependent upon a future outcome that might or might not occur. Referring in this publication to the practice of attorneys in charging their clients a fee contingent upon the financial outcome of the case. Investigators are not allowed to charge on contingency fee basis. Such fee agreement might prejudice or influence the outcome of an investigator's work.

Contract – A legally binding document between parties prescribing the anticipated obligations of each party. Contracts for investigative services are suggested as they reduce to a writing the obligations and expectations of all parties.

Credentials – A qualification or achievement either earned or awarded. Generally referring to a body of knowledge and experience.

Criminal – Related to an illegal act or activity.

Diligence – Careful and persistent work or effort.

Drone – A remotely controlled flying object frequently used for surveillance or photography.

Employee – A person working for wages or salary. Referring in this publication to an individual working for an investigator. That person might be an investigator, or part of administrative or other support staff.

Entrapment – To induce for the purpose of trapping, as in a crime. To suggest to someone that an action be committed when such activity would not have independently occurred to him or her. (See also: roping.)

Evidence – Information, physical materials, items pertinent to and applicable to establish facts in a legal investigation. That which is used as proof in a court of law.

Ex parte – For one party. At the request of or for one party only. Refers in this publication to communicating with one party in a litigation who is without benefit of counsel.

Fees – Moneys charged for services rendered. An investigators fees may be hourly or per assignment. They generally include mileage and expenses.

Friend – Used here to define being "asked" or "accepted" into the social media community that is separate and apart from a general posting for public view. A special status of one invited into the inner circle of one's social media communications.

Hacking – Gaining access to information stored on an electronic device such as a computer or cell telephone by persons without permission to do so. The illegal observation of private and confidential information. Breaking in.

In-house investigator – Working within a law firm, company or corporation as a salaried employee. An investigator with an employer-employee relationship with a company other than an investigative agency.

Internet – A global network of communication and information.

Integrity – A value structure of honesty and trustworthiness.

Knowingly – Aware, with knowledge, intentionally. Actual knowledge.

Law Enforcement – A branch of government burdened with the duty to maintain law and order. Agencies are specific to jurisdictions and communities. Comprised of police departments, sheriff's deputies, militia and other compensated enforcement arms of government.

License – Authorization. Having a permit; being allowed. Referring to authorization to do business as an investigator in jurisdictions that have licensing laws.

Litigation – Lawsuit or court matter. Action to make a determination through use of the court system.

Media – Referring to all reporters and journalists providing information and opinion to the public via radio, television, internet or written news sources.

Memorialize – Reduce to a writing, recording or visual image to preserve an event, action or utterance.

Misconduct – Acting in a manner that is inappropriate or unacceptable to the general mores, rules or regulations of a group.

Process Server – One who delivers documents from a court of law for the purpose of notification of a legal action.

Professional discretion – The freedom to decide what should be done in a particular situation, based upon experience and involvement in the profession.

Professional investigator – An individual duly licensed and authorized to conduct the business of investigation. One whose profession, business or industry is that of finding facts for others.

Reasonable – Using sound judgment. Fair and sensible. Acting in a manner that is prudent conduct for an investigator.

Records – Documents related to a case. History, paperwork, evidence and notes related to a case under investigation or that has been investigated.

Remuneration – Payment for a service. Providing a fee or value to another for that which they have done.

Retainer – Payment in advance to ensure the work of another. A pre-payment.

Roping – Setting a trap for. Inducing or enticing someone to perform an act that he or she would not normally perform. Used synonymously with entrapment in this publication. (See also: entrapment.)

Runner – A individual paid to obtain personal injury clients for an attorney. One who solicits clients for a lawyer. One who solicits clients for personal injury attorneys. Often referred to as ambulance chasers, a runner is generally reimbursed by way of a finder's fee and often by compensation after the settlement of personal injury litigation. Such practices are against the law of many states and punishable as criminal acts. (See also: capper.)

Security – A means of insuring safety. Used here to imply the protection by Investigators of their confidential data in the manner in which it is stored.

Social Media – Technology (internet and cellular communication) that allows for groups to be formed for the purpose of sharing information and ideas. Communications networks.

Solicitation – Attempt to obtain, advertise for or otherwise glean work from another party.

Subcontractor – An individual firm or company working for another. An investigator who is employed by another investigator as part of a larger project.

Subpoena – An order by the court to appear and testify or produce documentation.

Sub rosa – Covert investigations. Undercover investigations. Investigations that necessitate pretext or ruse to conceal the identity of the investigator.

Surveillance – Observation. Generally that which is performed by an investigator. Surveillance is primarily a covert action used as an investigative tool to report the activity of another person to a client.

Technology – Machinery and equipment developed from scientific advancements such as computers, internet, GPS, drones and tracking devices. Any scientifically based piece of equipment.

Termination – Ending. Cessation of a relationship. Used in this publication as the conclusion of a working relationship between an investigator and a client.

Tribunal – A court of law, an arbitration panel or other official body established to settle disputes.

Truth – One person's truth is not necessarily that of all persons. Bias or perspective can affect the interpretation of facts. The investigator must be diligent to understand the difference between truth and facts. Facts are incontrovertible. Truth is often subjective.

Truthfulness – Being accurate and honest. Providing real information. Not creating or fabricating wrong information.

Writing – That which is recorded in a document that can be referred to repeatedly. Used in this publication to indicate a written contract or agreement between parties.

Appendices

125

Professional Investigator State Licensing Authorities[1]

State	Licensing Required?	Licensing Authority
Alabama	Yes	Alabama Private Investigation Board (APIB) PO Box 241206, Montgomery, AL 36124
Alaska	Yes	City of Fairbanks, City Clerk's Office 800 Cushman St., Fairbanks, AK 99701 cityclerk@ci.fairbanks.ak.us
Arizona	Yes	Arizona Dept of Public Safety Licensing Unit PO Box 6828 MD1160, Phoenix, AZ 85005
Arkansas	Yes	Arkansas State Police One State Police Plaza Dr. Little Rock, AR 72209 info@asp.arkansas.gov
California	Yes	Bureau of Security & Investigative Services PO Box 989002 West Sacramento, CA 95798
Colorado	No	Colorado Office of Private Investigator Licensure has ended effective August 31, 2021, and licenses are no longer valid after that date.
Connecticut	Yes	Dept of Emergency Service & Public Protection Division of State Police
Delaware	Yes	Delaware State Police PO Box 430 Dover, DE 19903

State	Licensing Required?	Licensing Authority
Florida	Yes	Dept of Agriculture & Consumer Services, Division of Licensing 2520 North Monroe St Tallahassee, FL 32303
Georgia	Yes	Georgia Board of Private Detectives & Security Agencies 166 Pryor St, SW Atlanta, GA 30303
Hawaii	Yes	Board of Private Detectives and Guards DCCA, PVL Licensing PO Box 3469 Honolulu, HI 96801
Idaho	No	
Illinois	Yes	Illinois Department of Professional Regulation 320 West Washington St-3rd Fl Springfield, IL 62786
Indiana	Yes	Indiana Professional Licensing Agency 302 W Washington Street-#E034 Indianapolis, IN 46204
Iowa	Yes	Iowa Department of Public Safety Private Investigative Licensing Wallace State Office Bldg Des Moines, IA 50319 piinfo@dps.state.ia.us
Kansas	Yes	Kansas Bureau of Investigation Private Detective Licensing 1620 SW Tyler Topeka, Kansas 66612-1837

State	Licensing Required?	Licensing Authority
Kentucky	Yes	Public Protection Cabinet-Office of Occupations and Professions Board of Licensure for Private Investigators 911 Leawood Drive Frankfort, KY 40601
Louisiana	Yes	Louisiana State Board of Private Investigator Examiners 7414 Perkins Rd, Suite 120 Baton Rouge, LA70808
Maine	Yes	Maine State Police Licensing and Inspections Unit 164 Statehouse Station Augusta, ME 04330
Maryland	Yes	Department of State Police – Licensing Division 7751 Washington Blvd Jessup, MD 20794
Massachusetts	Yes	Department of State Police – Licensing Unit 485 Maple St Danvers, MA 01923
Michigan	Yes	Michigan Dept of Licensing & Regulatory Affairs PO Box 30018 Lansing, MI 48909
Minnesota	Yes	Minnesota Board of Private Detective & Protective Agent Services 445 Minnesota St., Suite 530 St. Paul, MN 55101
Mississippi	No	

State	Licensing Required?	Licensing Authority
Missouri	No	
Montana	Yes	Montana Dept of Labor & Industry Board of Private Security/Private Investigators 111 North Jackson Lower Level PO Box 200513 Helena, MT 59620
Nebraska	Yes	State of Nebraska, Secretary of State PO Box 94608 Lincoln, NE 68509-4508
Nevada	Yes	Nevada Private Investigator's Licensing Board 704 W Nye Lane, Suite 203 Carson City, Nevada 89703 pibinfo@ag.nv.gov
New Hampshire	Yes	New Hampshire State Police Support Services Bureau – Permits & Licensing Unit 10 Hazen Drive Concord, NH 03305
New Jersey	Yes	New Jersey Division of State Police Private Detective Unit PO Box 7068 West Trenton, NJ 08628
New Mexico	Yes	Department of Regulation and Licensing Toney Anaya Building 2550 Cerrillos Rd Santa Fe, NJ 87505
New York	Yes	New York State, Department of State Division of Licensing Services PO Box 2201 Albany, NY 12201-2001

State	Licensing Required?	Licensing Authority
North Carolina	Yes	North Carolina Private Protective Service Board PO Box 29500 3320 Old Garner Rd Raleigh, NC 27626
North Dakota	Yes	State of North Dakota Private Investigation and Security Board 513 Bismark Expwy – Suite 5 Bismark, ND 58504 NDPISB@Midco.net
Ohio	Yes	Ohio Private Investigation & Security Services Commission PISGS PO Box 182001 Columbus, OH 43218-2001
Oklahoma	Yes	Council on Law Enforcement Education & Training 2401 Egypt Road Ada, Oklahoma 74820-0669
Oregon	Yes	Oregon Board of Private Investigators 445 State Office Building 800 NE Oregon St #33 Portland, OR 97232
Pennsylvania	Yes	Licenses issued by Courts of Common Pleas Contact: Pennsylvania State Police 1800 Elmerton Ave Harrisburg, PA 17110 for exact county information

State	Licensing Required?	Licensing Authority
Rhode Island	Yes	Licenses issued by town or city –contact individual municipality for additional information
South Carolina	Yes	South Carolina Law Enforcement Division PO Box 21398 Columbia, SC 29221
South Dakota	No	
Tennessee	Yes	State of Tennessee-Department of Commerce & Insurance Division of Regulator Boards-Private Investigation Comm 500 James Robertson Parkway-2nd Floor Nashville, TN 37243
Texas	Yes	Texas Commission on Private Security PO Box 13509-Capital Station Austin, TX 78711
Utah	Yes	Utah Department of Public Safety 4501 South 2700 West Salt Lake City, UT 84119
Vermont	Yes	Office of Professional Regulation 89 Main Street 3rd Floor Montpelier, VT 05620-3401
Virginia	Yes	Commonwealth of Virginia Department of Criminal Justice Services PO Box 1300 Richmond, VA 23218
Washington	Yes	State of Washington Business Licensing Services PO Box 9034 Olympia, WA 98507-9034

State	Licensing Required?	Licensing Authority
West Virginia	Yes	West Virginia Secretary of State Building 1, Suite 157-K 1900 Kanawha Blvd. East Charleston, WV 25305 licensing@wvsos.com
Wisconsin	Yes	Wisconsin Department of Safety and professional Services PO Box 8935 Madison, WI 53708-8935 web@dsps.wi.gov
Wyoming	No	

---

[1] The Author recognizes P I Magazine for assistance in updating the charts in this section.

Professional Investigators Certifications

Source	Acronym	Certification	Acronym
American Society for Industrial Security	ASIS	Certified Protection Professional	CPP
American Society for Industrial Security	ASIS	Professional Certified Investigator	PCI
Association of Certified Fraud Examiners	ACFE	Certified Fraud Examiner	CFE
California Association of Licensed Investigators	CALI	Certified Professional Investigator	CPI
California Association of Licensed Investigators	CALI	Certified Security Professional	CSP
Criminal Defense Investigators	CDI	Board Certified Criminal Defense Investigator	CCDI
Florida Association of Licensed Investigators	FALI	Florida Certified Investigator	FCI
National Association of Legal Investigators	NALI	Certified Legal Investigator	CLI
INTELLENET	INTELLENET	Board Accredited Investigator	BAI
Source	Acronym	Certification	Acronym

Texas Association of Licensed Investigators	TALI	Texas Certified Investigator	TCI
Colleges and Universities	Currently programs are increasing nationwide	There are too many to include in this compendium	Check online for updates.

Professional Investigators Associations National and International

Acronym	Name	Country
AAPI	Alberta Association of Private Investigators	Canada
ABI	Association of British Investigators	United Kingdom
ACFE	Association of Certified Fraud Examiners	USA
ADPPP	Associcao de Detectives Privados Profissionals de Portugal	Portugal
AGPI	Association of German Private Investigators	Germany
AISP	Association of Investigators and Security Professionals	Australia
ASIS	American Society for Industrial Security	USA
CII	Council of International Investigators	International
CIPI	Certified Investigative Professionals, Inc.	USA
CNDDEEP	Coordination Nationale Des Detectives Et Enqueteurs Profesionnels	France
CPI	Council of Private Investigators	Canada – Ontario
FDDE	Association of Danish Detectives	Denmark

Acronym	Name	Country
FSPD	Fachverband Schweizerischer Privat Detektive	Switzerland
GIN	Global Investigators Network	International
IAPI	Italian Association of Private Investigators	Italy
IASIR	International Association of Security and Investigative Regulators	USA
IFPDISI	Italian Federation of Private Detectives, Investigators and Security Information	Italy
INTELLENET	International Intelligence Network	International
NALI	National Association of Legal Investigators	USA and International
NCISS	National Council of Investigative and Security Services	USA
PIABC	Alberta Association of Private Investigators	Canada – Alberta
SACCI	South African Council of Civil Investigations	South Africa
SAPI	Spanish Association of Private Investigators	Spain
WAD	World Association of Detectives	International
WAPI	World Association of Private Investigators	International

Professional Investigator Associations State

State	Acronym	Full Name
Alabama	APIA	Alabama Professional Investigator's Association
Alaska	AIA	Alaska Investigator's Association
Arizona	AALPIA	Arizona Association of Licensed Private Investigators
Arkansas	AAPI	Arkansas Association of Professional Private Investigators
Arkansas	PIAA	Private Investigator's Association of Arkansas
California	CALI	California Association of Licensed Investigators
California	PICA	Professional Investigators of California
Colorado	CSPI	Colorado Society of Private Investigators
Colorado	PPIAC	Professional Private Investigators Association of Colorado
Connecticut	CALPI	Connecticut Association of Licensed private Investigators
Delaware	DADA	Delaware Association of Detective Agencies
Florida	FAPI	Florida Association of Private Investigators
Florida	FALI	Florida Association of Licensed Investigators
Florida	PIA	Private Investigator's Association of Florida
Florida	SFIA	South Florida Investigators Association
Georgia	GAPPI	Georgia Association of Professional Private Investigators
Georgia	ISPAG	Investigative & Security Professional Association of Georgia
Idaho	PIAI	Private Investigators Association of Idaho

State	Abbr.	Association
Illinois	ADSAI	Associated Detectives & Security Agencies of Illinois, Inc.
Indiana	IAPI	Indiana Association of Professional Investigators
Indiana	INSPI	Indiana Society of Professional Investigators
Iowa	IAPI	Iowa Association of Private Investigators
Kansas	KAPI	Kansas Association of Private Investigators
Kansas	KALI	Kansas Association of Licensed Investigators
Kentucky	KPIA	Kentucky Professional Investigators Association
Kentucky	KSPI	Kentucky Society of Professional Investigators
Louisiana	LPIA	Louisiana Private Investigators Association
Maine	MLPIA	Maine Licensed Private Investigators Association
Maryland	MISA	Maryland Investigators & Security Association
Maryland	PIAM	Professional Investigators Alliance of Maryland
Massachusetts	LPDAM	Licensed Private Detectives Association of Massachusetts
Michigan	MCP	Michigan Council of Private Investigators
Minnesota	MAPI	Minnesota Association of Private Investigators
Mississippi	MPIA	Mississippi Professional Investigators Association
Missouri	MAPI	Missouri Association of Professional Investigators
Montana	MAPI	Montana Association of Private Investigators
Nebraska	NALPI	Nebraska Association of Licensed Private Investigators

Nevada	NSPI	Nebraska Association of Licensed Private Investigators
New Hampshire	NHLI	New Hampshire League of Investigators
New Jersey	NJLPIA	New Jersey Licensed Private Investigators Association, Inc.
New Mexico	PIANM	Private Investigators Association of New Mexico
New York	ALDONYS	Associated Licensed Detectives of New York State
New York	SPI	Society of Professional Investigators
North Carolina	NCAPI	North Carolina Association of Private Investigators
Ohio	OASIS	Ohio Association of Security and Investigative Services
Ohio	OIA	Ohio Investigators Association
Oklahoma	OPIA	Oklahoma Private Investigators Association
Oregon	OALI	Oregon Association of Licensed Investigators, Inc
Pennsylvania	PALI	Pennsylvania Association of Licensed Investigators
Puerto Rico	SPIPR	Society of Private Investigators of Puerto Rico
Rhode Island	LPDARI	Licensed Private Detectives Association of Rhode Island
South Carolina	SCALI	South Carolina Association of Legal Investigators
Tennessee	TPIA	Tennessee Professional Investigators Association
Tennessee	TAI	Tennessee Association of Investigators
Texas	TALI	Texas Association of Licensed Investigators
Texas	NTPIA	North Texas Private Investigators Association
Utah	PIAU	Private Investigators Association of Utah, Inc

Vermont	VAISS	Vermont Association of Investigative and Security Services
Virginia	PIAV	Private Investigators Association of Virginia
Virginia	PISA	Professional Investigators and Security Association
Washington	PNAI	Pacific Northwest Association of Investigators
Washington	WALI	Washington Association of Legal Investigators
West Virginia	PISPWV	Private Investigators and Security Professionals of West Virginia
Wisconsin	PAWLI	Professional Association of Wisconsin Licensed Investigators

Subject Guide to the Code of Professional Conduct

About the Author

KITTY HAILEY, CLI has always been passionate about her profession. She has dedicated her life to working actively as a private investigator. Simultaneously she strives to educate and enlighten other investigators to ways in which they can do their jobs with excellence and with ethics.

She has written voraciously for professional journals and has penned more than fifty (50) articles to instruct and inform new and experienced investigators. Kitty has contributed to several industry compilations including: _Advanced Forensic Civil Investigations, Advanced Forensic Criminal Investigations_ and _Corporate Investigations Volume I and Volume II._ She is the sole author of _The Professional Investigator Book One and Book Two_ and _Conversation with an Investigator._

This is the fourth edition of her seminal work on ethics for investigators. _Code of Professional Conduct: Standards and Ethics for the Investigative Profession_ which was first written in 2002 as a necessary addition to the lexicon of this profession. The _Code_ is being used by every major advanced certification program in the country and has been adopted by state and national associations as their own. Her LEGACY PROJECT is the continued push to have one standardized code of ethics for all investigators nationally. This will enhance the value of their work and ensure the highest professional conduct from all in the field of investigations.

Her work as a civil rights investigator and in the field of wrongful convictions has resulted in numerous persons being positively affected by her investigations. As part of several wonderful teams of dedicated men and women she has helped to walk more than twenty (20) persons off of death row and either back into general population or totally free from incarceration. Her civil rights work continues a fifty-year struggle to see equality in the treatment of all persons.

Kitty Hailey, CLI is the winner of numerous awards for her writing and her service. This year she was awarded the New Jersey Private Investigators Association *Meritorious Service Award*. She was named one of PI Magazines *Best Investigators for 2022* and is the recipient of the *Buddy Bombet Lifetime Achievement Award*. Additionally, Kitty was named one of Forbes magazines *"Fifty Women Over Fifty"* for *2022*; allowing her to be a mirror to reflect back upon the good works of all investigators.